THE LIMITS OF CRIMINAL LAW

INTERNATIONAL AND COMPARATIVE CRIMINAL JUSTICE

Series Editors:

Mark Findlay, *Institute of Criminology, University of Sydney, Australia*
Ralph Henham, *Nottingham Law School, Nottingham Trent University, UK*

This series explores the new and rapidly developing field of international and comparative criminal justice and engages with its most important emerging themes and debates. It focuses on three interrelated aspects of scholarship which go to the root of understanding the nature and significance of international criminal justice in the broader context of globalization and global governance. These include: the theoretical and methodological problems posed by the development of international and comparative criminal justice; comparative contextual analysis; the reciprocal relationship between comparative and international criminal justice and contributions which endeavor to build understandings of global justice on foundations of comparative contextual analysis.

Other titles in the series:

Domestic Deployment of the Armed Forces
Military Powers, Law and Human Rights
Michael Head and Scott Mann
ISBN 978 0 7546 7346 0

Democracy in the Courts
Lay Participation in European Criminal Justice Systems
Marijke Malsch
ISBN 978 0 7546 7405 4

The Disruption of International Organised Crime
An Analysis of Legal and Non-Legal Strategies
Angela Veng Mei Leong
ISBN 978 0 7546 7066 7

Restorative Justice
Ideals and Realities
Margarita Zernova
ISBN 978 0 7546 7032 2

The Limits of Criminal Law
A Comparative Analysis of Approaches to Legal Theorizing

CARL CONSTANTIN LAUTERWEIN
University of Munich, Germany

Routledge
Taylor & Francis Group
LONDON AND NEW YORK

First published 2010 by Ashgate Publishing

2 Park Square, Milton Park, Abingdon, Oxfordshire OX14 4RN
52 Vanderbilt Avenue, New York, NY 10017

Routledge is an imprint of the Taylor & Francis Group, an informa business

First issued in paperback 2020

British Library Cataloguing in Publication Data
Lauterwein, Carl Constantin.
The limits of criminal law : a comparative analysis of approaches to legal theorizing. -- (International and comparative criminal justice)
1. Criminal law--Interpretation and construction.
2. Criminal law--Australia. 3. Criminal law--Germany.
I. Title II. Series
345'.001-dc22

Library of Congress Cataloging-in-Publication Data
Lauterwein, Carl Constantin.
The limits of criminal law : a comparative analysis of approaches to legal theorizing / by Carl Constantin Lauterwein.
p. cm. -- (International and comparative criminal justice)
Includes bibliographical references and index.
ISBN 978-0-7546-7946-2 (hardback)
1. Criminal law--Philosophy. 2. Criminal justice, Administration of--Germany.
3. Criminal justice, Administration of--Australia. I. Title.

K5018.L38 2009
345--dc22

2009041633

ISBN 978-0-7546-7946-2 (hbk)
ISBN 978-0-367-60289-5 (pbk)

Contents

Foreword

Mark Findlay[1]

Comparative legal analysis has never been a convincing area of socio-legal scholarship. In no small measure this is due to the incapacity of lawyers to appreciate and activate deep contextual understandings prior to engaging the comparative endeavour. For some years now I have advocated the use of comparative contextual analysis to enliven a truly reflective commitment, at least when understanding the intersection between procedural traditions.[2] This book charts a similar course with theoretical foundations as its frame of reference.

However, theorizing criminal law across jurisdictions wherein the terrain and nature of theory and theorizing is differentially experienced can be fraught with difficulty. Without careful contextualization one is left comparing cheese and chalk, with the consequence that one person's theory is another's atheoretical or ahistorical justification.

The first challenge for this text was to 're-imagine' theory and theorizing in two very different legislative and political locations. The naïve intention was to cast an emergent federal common law jurisdiction against an established civil law tradition in order to critique the place of theory in two very different criminal laws. What became immediately apparent was the reality that theory is enunciated and invigorated in unique ways dependent on the purposes for determining criminal liability and imposing criminal sanctions. The operational relativity of criminal law, therefore, was as much a determinant of the nature of theory as it is a product of its influence.

The author initially anticipated a comparative enterprise little more than contrasting legal narrative so that theory would be revealed in different forms and with differential impacts, and out of distinct procedural and normative histories. This was not possible. Undaunted, the research developed a rich conversational methodology giving voice to important critics, practitioners and scholars who did much more than articulate the trajectory of theorizing against which a more documented theoretical tradition could be reflected. The result is a refreshing discourse on the veracity of theory in the criminal laws of Australia and Germany, as experienced in Australia by those who rationalize, argue and reformulate

1 Professor of Criminal Justice, Law School, University of Sydney; Professor of International Criminal Justice, Law School, University of Leeds.

2 For a discussion of this see Findlay, M. (1999) *The Globalisation of Crime*, Cambridge: Cambridge University Press.

criminal law, and in Germany by those who give legislative purchase to narrative doctrine.

Attempting sharp jurisdictional comparisons like those intended here is not without its risks. If the suggestion can be drawn that theory is devalued in one context because it is not revealed in legal narrative or prescribed in clear and consistent legislative form, then the comparative method needs refinement. The author is mindful of this. He has nuanced the 'conversations' about theorizing, against narrative theory particularly in contested social contexts where liability and sanction are situationally dependent. In turn, this does not deny a theoretical engagement on the measure of narrative and its understatement. In Australia, where there is a rich history of intersection between criminal law reform and criminology theorizing, criminal law is subtly (and not dogmatically) influenced by competing meta-theories of criminalization in its post colonial history. A contextual and dynamic approach to this comparative analysis enables the reader to appreciate the place of criminal law, and its theoretical foundations, in dealing with real-life problems and political agendas. In the German context similar problems and agendas reflect against codified doctrine, but are no less subject to the adaptability of the criminal law to modern times.

The controversial insights from the author's interviews show a powerful reflective spirit in a jurisdiction where the narrative of theorizing remains largely concealed. The critical evaluation of theory narrative in Germany is also enlivened through application of criminal law to contexts of radical social change. What we are left with is an insightful and socially grounded placement of theory in criminal law as it has been sometimes savagely instrumentalized for the political purposes of control above coherence.

Preface

When I told a fellow postgraduate student at Sydney Law School about my being quite astonished by the lack of an academic discussion on the legitimate limits of criminal law in Australia, he made a remarkable statement. He said that it was his impression that while law was seen as a *science* in Germany, in English-speaking countries it was regarded as being an *art*.

I believe there is much to learn from this summary of the different approaches, notwithstanding the fact that it is a common platitude amongst German practising lawyers to regard law as a *craft* instead of a science. The everyday work of a practising lawyer may indeed have more in common with the job of a craftsman than that of a scientist. But the same may also be said of a doctor, and no one would reason that medicine was merely a craft. What my fellow student meant and what will be the general theme of this book is the *academic* understanding of the nature of the subject: the approach to law taken by scholars and, resulting from that, the way in which law students are educated and how this influences the practising lawyers' understanding of their field of profession.

This book is the result of the fact that I was fortunate enough to have the great privilege of gaining first-hand experience of both approaches by studying law in both Germany and Australia. Despite focusing on the limits of criminal law, it is my strong belief that many of my findings also apply to other fields of the law, if not the general understanding of legal education and the role of lawyers in both countries. The limits of criminal law are, however, probably the most suitable example to illustrate these differences since the question of the legitimate scope of the criminal law concerns the most severe means of power which a state can exercise over its citizens.

For providing me with most valuable insights into the differences between the German and the Australian way of thinking, studying, researching and practising law, I would like to thank Professor Alex Ziegert. Although Alex is not a criminal lawyer, being able to discuss the project in German with someone who is familiar with both legal systems was a priceless advantage. Furthermore, the fact that Alex specializes in sociology of law provided for an additional perspective that proved to be very valuable.

Many thanks go to Professor Mark Findlay, who was always available to help solve whatever problems arose – including at times when he had far more severe problems to deal with himself. Mark is an outstanding figure in Australian criminal law and his knowledge, experience and contacts were the most valuable asset I could think of for my research in Australia and the comparison with the German approach. I am also very grateful for him providing the Foreword to the book.

Finally, my sincere gratitude goes to the 11 Australian criminal law experts who agreed to be interviewed. Without their willingness to answer what were at times uncomfortable questions, edit and approve their transcripts and to consent to being identified when citing their statements (which 10 out of 11 did), this book could not have been written.

Abbreviations

Bt-Drs.	*Bundestagsdrucksache* (German Federal Parliament printed paper)
BtMG	*Gesetz über den Umgang mit Betäubungsmitteln* (German Narcotics Act)
BVerfG	*Bundesverfassungsgericht* (German Federal Constitutional Court)
BVerfGE	*Entscheidungen des Bundesverfassungsgerichts* (Collection of the judgements of the Federal Constitutional Court)
GG	*Grundgesetz* (German Constitution; literally translated Basic Law)
m.n.	marginal number
NJW	*Neue Juristische Wochenschrift* (New Weekly Law Journal)
OWiG	*Gesetz über Ordnungswidrigkeiten* (Administrative Offences Act)
JR	*Juristische Rundschau* (Law Review Journal)
NStZ	*Neue Zeitschrift für Strafrecht* (New Criminal Law Journal)
JuS	*Juristische Schulung* (Journal of Legal Education)
StGB	*Strafgesetzbuch* (German Criminal Code)
StPO	*Strafprozessordnung* (German Code of Criminal Procedure)

Chapter 1
Law, Limits and Legitimacy – Germany and Australia

> But the real problem is that lawyers are not trained or even encouraged to examine the role of law in society and to assess how well the legal system is functioning. They are trained and encouraged to regard the law as an ancient set of principles – without social, political or economic content – that can solve any problem, present or future, if only they are correctly applied. It is a fantasy that admits of deficiencies in every other aspect of society but not in the law.[1]

> Criminal law theory, which consists of scientifically ordered doctrines on the existence and the functions of criminal law, has always had justified reasons to look at the diversity of criminal law and to reflect on changes in the criminal law.[2]

Law has limits. This undoubtedly general statement raises the question: which law and which limits are we talking about? This book deals with the limits of criminal law. More precisely, it deals with the substantive part of the criminal law, which is the area that defines certain behaviours as offences and imposes punishment on persons who commit such offences. The 'limits' analysed in this work concern what kinds of conduct are criminalized.

It is another generalization to say that, while some conduct is criminal in every given society, many forms of behaviour are criminalized in some countries, but are not punishable in others. Thus, the limits of criminal law are dependent on the law as it stands in a particular jurisdiction. But it is not the intention of this book to compare the current content of the substantive criminal law in different countries. Indeed, the criminal law as it stands is not the subject here at all.

As laws, including laws defining criminal offences, are made by the state, another perspective on the limits concerns the lawmaker. What can be made criminal by the state and what cannot? In a constitutional state, this question itself is answered by laws; laws that regulate legislation may set limits for the state in this regard. These limits emanate from constitutions as well as international

1 Michael Sexton and Laurence W. Maher, *The Legal Mystique: The Role of Lawyers in Australian Society* (Angus & Robertson Publishers, Sydney 1982) 180.

2 Winfried Hassemer, 'Vielfalt und Wandel. Offene Horizonte eines interkulturellen Strafrechts' in Otfried Höffe (ed.), *Gibt es ein interkulturelles Strafrecht?* (Suhrkamp, Frankfurt a.M. 1999) 157. English translations of the German titles are provided in the bibliography.

and supranational laws. This, again, leads to major differences between different jurisdictions in this respect. But it is not the intention of this book to examine the different legal limits for criminal lawmakers in different countries either.

Aside from legal limitations to the scope of the substantive criminal law, there is another criterion that can be considered. One can also question whether the criminalization of certain forms of behaviour is *legitimate*. In contrast to legality, legitimacy is a purely theoretical category, and the criteria used to identify whether something is legitimate cannot be found in the law itself, but must be reasoned separately. This independence from the law provides for an interesting feature: the question can be treated identically in different countries, despite the diversity of the substantive laws in force. In Germany, the answer to this question is commonly given by invoking the theory known as the *Rechtsgutstheorie*, while in English-speaking countries the harm principle is often referred to for this purpose.

Therefore, in German discussions it is commonly assumed that the harm principle is the Anglophone equivalent to the *Rechtsgutstheorie* in this regard. The works of English and American scholars like Andrew Ashworth and Joel Feinberg are regarded in Germany as proving this assumption. Indeed, comparing these approaches to the *Rechtsgutstheorie* one easily finds similarities. The original version of the harm principle, as it was formulated by John Stuart Mill in particular, features several characteristics that are also part of the German approach – regarding both the foundations and the conclusions of the theories. On the other hand, the *Rechtsgutstheorie* seems to hold a unique position with regard to its degree of acceptance and influence in German academic writing and, in particular, in legal education. While this seems to be true when compared with any jurisdiction that is based on the common law tradition, it is particularly the case with regard to Australia.

It is easy to see that the criminal law systems of Australia and Germany are very different, just by looking at the common law tradition on the one hand and the continental civil law system on the other, and the fact that Australian criminal law is largely governed by state legislation while criminal law is almost entirely a federal power in Germany, and only some Australian states have a criminal code. It is, on the other hand, not quite so obvious why Australian academics do not engage – at least not visibly – in normative discussion on general legitimate limits of the criminal law. In contrast to the United States and the United Kingdom, there is no Australian author to whose work the *Rechtsgutstheorie* could be compared.

Taking the *Rechtsgut* concept as a starting point, the purpose of this book is to analyse how the question 'What sorts of conduct may the state legitimately make criminal?' is dealt with in Australia, which is a country in which the whole system of criminal law operates completely differently to that of Germany but which, despite the lack of a Bill of Rights, is also characterized by a liberal constitutional order that is governed by the rule of law.

Chapter 2 presents the German approach. Setting out the German concept provides a starting point for discussion, as well as a model for comparison with the Australian perspective. In addition to laying down the *Rechtsgut* concept's function for questions regarding legal theory, its impact on the practical application of the current criminal law will be illustrated within an excursus.

In order to present the Australian perspective, it was necessary to significantly alter the methodology used in the analysis from that originally planned. As set out in Chapter 3, interviews with 11 Australian criminal law experts were conducted and evaluated. Despite the fact that this was done due to a lack of a comprehensive discussion on the topic in the Australian literature, this approach turned out to provide a unique insight into the reasons for the current Australian understanding.

In Chapter 4, the results of the interviews are considered together with the existing literature in order to analyse the Australian perspective. As will be seen in the comparison with the *Rechtsgutstheorie*, the German and Australian approaches differ significantly with regard to the methodology applied. After analysing the reasons for this divergence, it will be argued that the Australian approach is descriptive in nature and suffers from a 'normative flaw' which is due to an emphasis on criminology rather than jurisprudence.

How the Australian approach deals with the legitimacy of particular offences is illustrated in Chapter 5 by using as examples three criminal offences that are all subject to critique by the German theory.

Finally, Chapter 6 presents the conclusions arising from the analysis. It is argued that the 'normative flaw' in the current Australian approach actually provides a unique opportunity for Australian criminal law scholarship.

Before the German *Rechtsgutstheorie* is presented in the next chapter, one point, which is crucial to the understanding of this analysis as a whole, must be made clear. As previously mentioned, the topic of this book is legal theory. Neither in Germany nor in Australia is the criminal law as it stands the product of a sophisticated theory. The theories that will be investigated here exist alongside the law in force. As we will see, they may influence the law, but the law itself is never the product of any theory.

If you are asking yourself at this point what the purpose of such theories is if not to produce law, you most likely come from the English-speaking legal tradition. If, on the other hand, you are asking yourself why this obvious point requires making at all, you are probably familiar with the continental legal system. This fundamental difference between the German and Australian approaches to theory will be a recurrent theme throughout the whole book, and one of the aims of the analysis is to narrow this gap in the understanding of criminal law theory. Despite focusing on the limits of criminal law, the book therefore aims to provide a wider comparative analysis of general legal theorizing.

Chapter 2
The German *Rechtsgutstheorie*

The criminalization of behaviour that cannot refer to a *Rechtsgut* would be state terror.[1]

The aim of this chapter is to provide an insight into the way in which German scholars answer the question 'What sorts of behaviour may the state legitimately make criminal?' The chapter does not seek to be comprehensive, but rather to demonstrate the main characteristics of the approach taken by the vast majority of German criminal lawyers, in order to provide a model to which the Australian perspective can be compared. It will be concluded that, despite many disputes with respect to details, the approach favoured in Germany provides lawyers with a dogmatic tool for legislative critique, which enables them to articulate critical views on legislative decisions in criminal law within the framework of a common matrix of argumentation.

The Function of Criminal Law

'The function of the criminal law is the protection of legal goods/interests' (*Aufgabe des Strafrechts ist der Schutz von Rechtsgütern*). This statement, or similar, can be found in almost every German criminal law textbook (on the general part[2]) and commentary on the Criminal Code (*Strafgesetzbuch* or StGB).[3] Of course, as

1 Winfried Hassemer, 'Darf es Straftaten geben, die ein strafrechtliches Rechtsgut nicht in Mitleidenschaft ziehen?' in Roland Hefendehl, Andrew von Hirsch and Wolfgang Wohlers (eds), *Die Rechstgutstheorie: Legitimationsbasis des Strafrechts oder dogmatisches Glasperlenspiel?* (Nomos, Baden-Baden 2003) 57, 64. Hassemer is a professor of legal theory, sociology of law, criminal law and law of criminal procedure. Until 7 May 2008 he was also Vice-President of the German Federal Constitutional Court (*Bundesverfassungsgericht* or BVerfG).

2 German criminal law texts deal either with the general part of criminal law or with the special part. The former concerns rules and principles that apply to every offence, while the latter concerns individual offences.

3 See, for example, Claus Roxin, *Strafrecht, Allgemeiner Teil, Band I: Grundlagen, Aufbau der Verbrechenslehre* (4th edn C.H. Beck, Munich 2006) 10; Hans-Joachim Rudolphi, 'Kommentierung zu § 1 StGB' in Hans-Joachim Rudolphi, Eckhard Horn and Erich Samson (eds), *Systematischer Kommentar zum Strafgesetzbuch, Band 1, Allgemeiner Teil, §§ 1-79b* (7th edn Luchterhand, Neuwied 2008) Vor § 1 m.n. 2; Herbert Tröndle and Thomas Fischer, *Strafgesetzbuch und Nebengesetze* (50th edn C.H. Beck, Munich 2001) Vor § 1 m.n. 1; Johannes Wessels and Werner Beulke, *Strafrecht, Allgemeiner Teil, Die Straftat und ihr*

with almost any question in law, and especially legal theory, this opinion is not unchallenged. There are a few scholars who do not agree with this concept and, particularly in recent times, criticism of the concept is increasing.[4] But in contrast to many other issues, the concept of the *Rechtsgutstheorie* is accepted, used and taught by the vast majority of German criminal law scholars.[5]

Although the concept itself is well established, the details of the theory are heavily disputed.[6] This is easy to understand as the statement 'the function of the criminal law is the protection of legal goods/interests' is rather meaningless unless the crucial term 'legal good/interest' has been defined. But the definition of the term *Rechtsgut* (legal good/interest) is everything but undisputed[7] – which is also why it is so hard to provide an English translation for the term.[8] 'Neither in the American nor in the English dogmatic or theory of criminal law is the term – or an equivalent synonym of it – in use.'[9] Obviously, this is also true for Australia.

Aufbau (38th edn C.F. Müller, Heidelberg 2008) 2; Wolfgang Joecks, 'Kommentierung zu § 1 StGB' in Wolfgang Joecks and Klaus Miebach (eds), *Münchener Kommentar zum Strafgesetzbuch* (C.H. Beck, Munich 2003) 12 et seq.; Volker Krey, *Deutsches Strafrecht, Allgemeiner Teil, Band 1, Grundlagen, Tatbestandsmäßigkeit, Rechtswidrigkeit, Schuld* (3rd edn Kohlhammer, Stuttgart 2008) 10; Adolf Schönke, Horst Schröder and Theodor Lenckner (eds), *Strafgesetzbuch: Kommentar* (27th edn C.H. Beck, Munich 2006) 152 et seq.; Rolf Schmidt, *Strafrecht, Allgemeiner Teil, Grundlagen der Strafbarkeit, Aufbau des strafrechtlichen Gutachtens* (6th edn Verlag Rolf Schmidt, Grasberg 2007) 1.

4 One of the most prominent critics of the concept is Günter Stratenwerth. See, for example, Günter Stratenwerth and Lothar Kuhlen, *Strafrecht, Allgemeiner Teil, Band 1, Die Straftat* (5th edn Heymanns, Cologne, Berlin, Munich 2004). For a different approach see also Knut Amelung, *Rechtsgüterschutz und Schutz der Gesellschaft* (Athenäum, Frankfurt a.M. 1972). Also see the different approaches presented in Roland Hefendehl, Andrew von Hirsch and Wolfgang Wohlers (eds), *Die Rechtsgutstheorie: Legitimationsbasis des Strafrechts oder dogmatisches Glasperlenspiel?* (Nomos, Baden-Baden 2003).

5 For what is apparently the only available English-language introduction to the *Rechtsgut* concept see Markus D. Dubber 'Theories of Crime and Punishment in German Criminal Law' (2006) 53 *American Journal of Comparative Law* 679.

6 Hence the heading of the section: 'The Debate on the Rechtsgut Concept' (*Der Streit um den Rechtsgutsbegriff*) in Roxin, *Allgemeiner Teil, Band I*, above n 3, 14.

7 Ibid.

8 Literally, the term consists of two nouns, law (*Recht*) and good (*Gut*) and means 'good of the law'. The translation sometimes found in the English literature is 'legal interest'; it is therefore not a mere translation, but more of a definition, since the word 'interest' – as is also the case in German – is a possible description of what a good (*Gut*) can be (see pp. 26–28 for details). To avoid defining the term instead of merely translating it, it will be referred to here as 'legal good/interest' or *Rechtsgut* (the plural of which is *Rechtsgüter*).

9 Andrew von Hirsch, 'Der Rechtsgutsbegriff und das "Harm Principle"' in Roland Hefendehl, Andrew von Hirsch and Wolfgang Wohlers (eds), *Die Rechtsgutstheorie: Legitimationsbasis des Strafrechts oder dogmatisches Glasperlenspiel?* (Nomos, Baden-Baden 2003) 13.

There is extensive German literature on the *Rechtsgutstheorie* and numerous different definitions and views are available.[10] However, in order to provide an insight into the German discussion, it is sufficient to use one concept of *Rechtsgüterschutz* (the protection of legal goods/interests) as an example which can then serve as a model for the analysis of the Australian perspective. For the purposes of this book, the general concept need not be comprehensively analysed and scrutinized as it is used only as an example of a way in which the question of the legitimate limits of the criminal law can be addressed and as a model to which the Australian understanding can be compared.[11]

The concept of *Rechtsgüterschutz* presented here is that developed by Claus Roxin.[12] Roxin, an emeritus professor of criminal law, criminal procedure and legal theory, wrote (in addition to many other well-known 'classics' in German criminal law[13]) the most comprehensive textbook on the general part of the substantive criminal law in Germany. It consists of two volumes of 1,100 and 900 pages in length respectively and is probably the most famous criminal law text in Germany.[14] Roxin's concept was chosen to serve as a model for the analysis because of the exceptional reputation of his criminal law textbook in Germany and the very detailed description of his theory provided in his text. Furthermore, it represents the mainstream of German scholarly opinion on this topic. Given purpose of this chapter, the structure of the following explanation of the concept closely follows that of Roxin's text. In this manner not only the substance of Roxin's concept of *Rechtsgüterschutz*, but also the *way* in which the issue is typically presented in German textbooks, can be included in the comparison.

---

10 The latest comprehensive publication on the current problems the concept faces is Hefendehl, von Hirsch and Wohlers (eds), above n 4. See also Roland Hefendehl, 'Mit langem Atem: Der Begriff des Rechtsguts – Oder: Was seit dem Erscheinen des Sammelbandes über die Rechtsgutstheorie geschah' (2007) *Goltdammers Archiv für Strafrecht* 1.

11 For a detailed description of the methodology used, see Chapter 3 below.

12 First presented in Claus Roxin, 'Sinn und Grenzen staatlicher Strafe' (1966) *Juristische Schulung* 377, 381–382.

13 For example Claus Roxin, *Strafverfahrensrecht* (25th edn C.H. Beck, Munich 1998); Claus Roxin, *Täterschaft und Tatherrschaft* (6th edn de Gruyter, Berlin 2006, first published 1963); Claus Roxin and Hans Achenbach, *Strafprozessrecht* (16th edn C.H. Beck, Munich 2006); Claus Roxin, *Höchstrichterliche Rechtsprechung zum Allgemeinen Teil des Strafrechts, 100 Entscheidungen für Studium und Referendariat mit Fragen und Antworten* (C.H. Beck, Munich 1998). The only English translation of one of Roxin's texts is a remarkable piece on the issues that stem from the understanding of criminal law being a social science on the one hand and a branch of jurisprudence on the other: Claus Roxin, 'Crime Policy and the Criminal Law System' (translated by J. Fosberry) in Institute for Scientific Co-operation (ed.), *Law and State, A Biannual Collection of Recent German Contributions to these Fields, Volume 6* (Göbel, Tübingen 1972) 32.

14 The fourth and latest edition of the first volume, in which the *Rechtsgutstheorie* is also discussed, was published in 2006. Roxin, *Allgemeiner Teil, Band I*, above n 3.

The Concept Developed by Claus Roxin

The first chapter of Roxin's text deals with The Criminal Law in the Formal Sense (*Das Strafrecht im formellen Sinn*). Here he explains the system of sanctions, the sources of criminal law and the substantive criminal law in its relationships with the law of procedure, laws dealing with the assessment of penalty and the execution of sentences, juvenile penal law and criminology. Finally, the subject of the text is presented: the general part of the substantive criminal law.[15]

After this introduction, Chapter 2 deals with The Substantive Concept of Crime (*Der materielle Verbrechensbegriff*)[16] by way of contrast to the formal approach presented in Chapter 1. It begins with the explanation that a substantive theory of crime cannot be extracted from the law as it stands, but must be considered detached from and prior to the current criminal law. 'It is a concept that provides the legislature with a rule for criminal policy – it explains what can be criminalized and what must not.'[17]

The fundamental claim of the *Rechtsgutstheorie* is that this substantive concept of crime arises from the function of the criminal law, which, it is argued, is 'the subsidiary protection of legal goods/interests' (*subsidiärer Rechtsgüterschutz*).[18] The subsidiarity of the criminal law is easily established – as criminal law is the most severe means to interfere with citizens, it should be used as a last resort.[19] The protection of legal goods/interests (*Rechtsgüterschutz*), however, is a concept which has to be reasoned more comprehensively.

The term *Rechtsgut* was first introduced by the German lawyer Birnbaum in 1834.[20] Although it is in dispute whether the term was originally used to limit the scope of the criminal law,[21] it has definitely been used in this sense since the end of the Nazi regime in Germany.

Today, the concept of *Rechtsgut* has two functions.[22] First, as acknowledged in both academia and practice, it is crucial for statutory interpretation of criminal laws. An interpretation of a law creating a criminal offence must consider what *Rechtsgut* is protected by the law. This is the only way in which the intention of Parliament when passing the provision in question can be considered.[23] This function of the *Rechtsgut* concept is referred to as the 'methodological' approach

---

15 The general part of the substantive criminal law is regulated by §§ 1–79b StGB.

16 The chapter is 54 pages in length.

17 Roxin, *Allgemeiner Teil, Band I*, above n 3, 14–15.

18 Ibid.

19 The German Federal Constitutional Court (*Bundesverfassungsgericht* or BVerfG) termed the criminal law the *ultimo ratio* of social policy. BVerGE 39, 47.

20 Johann Michael Franz Birnbaum, 'Über das Erfordernis einer Rechtsverletzung zum Begriff des Verbrechens' (1834) (15) *Archiv des Criminalrechts* 149.

21 Amelung, above n 4, denies this.

22 See also von Hirsch, above n 9.

23 See also the common law purposive approach to interpretation, for example Catriona Cook et al., *Laying Down the Law* (6th edn LexisNexis, Chatswood 2005) 214–224.

to the term. During the Nazi regime in Germany, the methodological approach was favoured, as it does not limit the legislature in its capacity to criminalize conduct, but merely provides a method of interpreting the law in a purposive way – whatever its purpose – and accordingly whatever the protected *Rechtsgut* – might be.[24]

Secondly, and far more importantly with regard to legal theory, the concept of *Rechtsgut* has a function related to criminal policy. If the function of the criminal law is the protection of legal goods/interests, then, it is argued, logically, *only* legal goods/interests may be protected by the criminal law.[25] In other words, the legislature must not criminalize any behaviour that does not harm or endanger a *Rechtsgut*. This function is called *systemkritisch*[26] (critical of the system) or *gesetzgebungskritisch*[27] (critical of the legislation), as it aims to establish limits on the legislature regarding criminal policy and therefore provides a framework for critical analysis of legislative practice.

In order to understand this second function of the *Rechtsgut* concept, two questions must be answered. On the one hand, one has to ask why the legislature should be limited at all in deciding to criminalize certain conduct, especially today when legislation is not made by an absolute monarch, but instead by a democratically legitimated Parliament. On the other hand, one has to ask what a *Rechtsgut* actually is, as without a definition of the term the whole concept is meaningless.

In relation to the first question, Roxin refers, as already mentioned, to the function of criminal law. He argues that the object of the criminal law is to enable citizens to cohabit in freedom and peace whilst all constitutionally guaranteed civil rights are assured.[28] Roxin's concept is based on a liberal understanding of the state founded on a social contract, although he does not discuss the many different variations on the social contract model found in political philosophy. In fact, he does not even mention the fact that there are different concepts.[29] For his purposes, the differences between the models are insignificant. He states:

---

24 How the methodological function of the *Rechtsgut* concept influences today's criminal law is illustrated in an excursus pp. 30 et seq.

25 See Hassemer, 'Darf es Straftaten geben', above n 1, 64.

26 Winfried Hassemer, *Theorie und Soziologie des Verbrechens. Ansätze zu einer praxisorientierten Rechtsgutslehre* (Athenäum, Frankfurt a.M. 1973).

27 Roxin, *Allgemeiner Teil, Band I*, above n 3, 18. Roxin argues that the concept was not critical of the existing system as a whole, but only of legislative acts within this system.

28 Roxin, *Allgemeiner Teil, Band I*, above n 3, 16; Roxin, 'Sinn und Grenzen', above n 13, 381–382.

29 As Roxin refers to the Enlightenment, he obviously means the models of Thomas Hobbes, John Locke and Jean-Jacques Rousseau. See also Carl Constantin Lauterwein, *Symbolische Gesetzgebung: Eine Untersuchung am Beispiel Strafrecht* (Voegel, Munich 2006) 22–25.

> One therefore acts on the hypothetical assumption that all the inhabitants of a certain territory enter into an agreement in which they consign to certain institutions the role of safeguarding their cohabitation. They create an organization – the state – and assign the right to safeguard the citizens by enacting criminal laws and other regulations to it. But since a criminal law restricts the individual in his or her liberty of action, nothing that is not necessary to achieve a peaceful and liberal co-existence may be prohibited. That therewith human dignity, equality and the other civil rights have to be respected is also a result of Enlightenment thinking, which considers these guarantees as essential conditions for human freedom.[30]

The answer to the second question of what a *Rechtsgut* actually is then follows from the answer to the first question. Roxin defines a *Rechtsgut* as:

> All facts or established goals that are necessary for the free personality development of the individual, the realization of his or her civil rights and the functioning of a political system which is based on these objectives.[31]

Consequences of the Concept

Roxin describes nine consequences arising from his concept of *Rechtsgut*:[32]

Arbitrary, Ideologically motivated Criminal Laws and Criminal Laws which Violate Civil Rights do not Protect Rechtsgüter That such laws, which violate principles such as equality, freedom of opinion or freedom of faith, are illegitimate is not in dispute. But those extreme cases are very rare in a constitutional state and the opponents of the *Rechtsgutstheorie* would come to the same conclusion.

A Description of Legal Objectives is Insufficient to Constitute a Rechtsgut which Legitimates a Criminal Offence Here, Roxin uses the very controversial offence of purchase and possession of marijuana for the purpose of self-administration[33] as an example. This offence is often legitimated by an argument that the protected *Rechtsgut* is the existence of a drug-free society. But Roxin insists that the

---

30 Roxin, *Allgemeiner Teil, Band I*, above n 3, 16–17.

31 Ibid. A definition which is similar but more intimately linked with the Constitution is developed in Lauterwein, above n 29, 25: '*Rechtsgüter* are functional units, which are guaranteed by the constitutional order to enable the individual's free personality development.'

32 Roxin, *Allgemeiner Teil, Band I*, above n 3, 18–29.

33 § 29(1) Nr. 3 of the Narcotics Act (*Gesetz über den Verkehr mit Betäubungsmitteln* or BtMG): 'A term of imprisonment of not more than five years or a fine shall be imposed upon anyone who possesses narcotics without holding a written permit to acquire them at the same time.'

punishability of this act cannot be defended by this reasoning as the crucial question of whether the criminalized behaviour affects the peaceful coexistence of the people and causes harm has not been answered. The construction of such a *Rechtsgut* (a drug-free society) is nothing more than the description of the offence's objective and therefore only conforms to a methodological concept of *Rechtsgut*. It does not satisfy the *systemkritische* (critical of the system) concept of *Rechtsgut*.

Immorality, Unethical or Other Reprehensible Conduct of Itself does not Constitute Harm to a Rechtsgut The prime example is homosexual conduct, which was a criminal offence for male persons in Germany until 1969. During the criminal law reform process of the 1960s and 1970s, the German Federal Parliament (*Bundestag*) at first resisted decriminalizing homosexual conduct by arguing that the legislature could criminalize 'particularly unethical conduct, which is considered to be shameful in the public opinion'[34] even when no *Rechtsgut* is harmed.

The decriminalization of homosexual conduct in the final stage of the criminal law reform in the late 1960s is considered to be the greatest victory achieved by the application of the *Rechtsgut* concept. Parliament's draft reforms were challenged by a group of 14 criminal law professors,[35] who published alternative drafts. One of these alternative drafts, published in 1968, dealt with sexual offences and had major influence on the decriminalization of homosexual conduct by promoting the *Rechtsgut* concept as providing the limit of legitimate criminalization related to sexual conduct.

Roxin acknowledges that opponents of the concept argue that decriminalization was based on a change of moral views in society rather than on the *Rechtsgut* concept. But he appropriately points out that the conclusion drawn from the *Rechtsgutstheorie* also applies to other conduct which is still immoral by today's standards, for example adultery and bestiality. In spite of still being generally considered immoral, both adultery and bestiality were decriminalized during the reform and the legislature decided to reform all sexual offences. Further, because of the critique based on the *Rechtsgut* concept in the alternative drafts, sexual offences were restricted to the prohibition of conduct affecting the sexual self-determination of others and the protection of young people.[36] The heading of Chapter 13 of the StGB was changed from Crimes against Morality to Crimes against Sexual Self-Determination, which also indicates an intention to limit punishability in this area to the protection of legal goods/interests.

The Violation of One's Own Dignity or the 'Dignity of Humankind' is not Sufficient to Justify Criminalization Roxin considers human dignity to be one of the most

---

34 BT-Drs. IV/650, 376.

35 One of whom was Roxin.

36 An inconsistent exception being the offence of incest, § 173 StGB, which was not abolished. See below pp. 15–16 and 94 et seq. for details.

important legal goods/interests.[37] However he does not approve of the violation of one's own dignity being used to justify criminalization. Such a use of the term human dignity, Roxin explains, is similar to the use of the concept of immorality in former times. For example, saying that sexual conduct with animals violates the human dignity of the person involved does not provide a reason to criminalize the behaviour. Similarly, considering suicide to be disrespectful to one's own dignity cannot justify criminalizing attempted suicide.[38]

Similarly, violation of 'the dignity of humankind' cannot be the basis of criminalization, since – even if something like the dignity of humankind exists – its violation has no impact on the safety and liberty of individuals.

The Protection of Feelings can only be Acknowledged as a Rechtsgut if the Feelings are of Threat In general, the protection of feelings is not considered to be the criminal law's function.[39] 'The function of the criminal law is the maintenance of human coexistence – not of human co-sentiment.'[40] Roxin draws a line at the point at which an individual feels affected in his or her feeling of safety, because peaceful and free coexistence implies that one does not have to fear others or be discriminated against by them. This is the basis for the criminalization of libel and slander,[41] as well as for punishing acts of demanding[42] or approving[43] severe crimes and also the vilification of religion and religious organizations.[44]

With regard to the protection of feelings, Roxin views the criminalization of acts of exhibitionism[45] critically. The safety aspect only legitimates criminalization of such acts in so far as they are committed in circumstances which will result in fear of a sexual assault. With respect to acts which would merely cause feelings of disgust or shame, he recommends an administrative offence instead of a criminal charge.

Finally, Roxin argues that the offence of grave desecration[46] cannot be legitimated through the protected good/interest of respect for the deceased and

37 Article 1 of the German Constitution (*Grundgesetz* or GG) states that human dignity is inviolable.

38 Although a literal interpretation of § 212 StGB (manslaughter) would allow for the punishability of attempted suicide (the section refers to one 'who kills a man', not 'another man'), it is undisputed that attempted suicide is not punishable in Germany. This is because the *Rechtsgut* that the offence protects is considered to be the life of *another* person.

39 See also Tatjana Hörnle, 'Der Schutz von Gefühlen im StGB' in Roland Hefendehl, Andrew von Hirsch and Wolfgang Wohlers (eds), *Die Rechstgutstheorie: Legitimationsbasis des Strafrechts oder dogmatisches Glasperlenspiel?* (Nomos, Baden-Baden 2003) 268.

40 Amelung, above n 4, 347.

41 §§ 185–200 StGB.

42 § 111 StGB.

43 § 140 StGB.

44 § 166 StGB.

45 § 183 StGB.

46 § 168 StGB.

their final resting place, as is the prevailing opinion in Germany. This would mean the mere protection of a feeling. According to Roxin, the reason for criminalization arises from the fact that also after death every human being has a right to respectful and dignified treatment. Therefore, the human dignity of a person would already be violated before death if they had to assume that after dying their grave would be defiled or their corpse would be stolen or bashed.[47]

Deliberate Self-harm and/or its Enabling and Support do not Legitimate Criminalization This consequence means that paternalism, in general, is not considered a legitimate argument for criminalization. The criminal law shall only prevent danger or harm that is inflicted upon a person against his or her will. What happens in accordance with the will of the 'victim' does not harm a *Rechtsgut*, but is an aspect of the individual's self-determination which is of no concern to the state.

The only legitimate exception to this rule against interfering with individual self-determination arises from deficiencies in the autonomy of the person concerned.[48] These deficiencies could be based on factors such as mental disorder, coercion, mistake, being underage or similar. Roxin argues that the controversial offence of homicide upon request[49] can be legitimated because the existential and irreversible character of suicide means that the sincerity and voluntariness of the will to die can only be manifested with sufficient clarity by killing oneself by one's own hand.[50]

The main and most discussed problem related to self-endangerment concerns drug laws. Roxin again uses as an example the offence of purchase and possession of marijuana for the purpose of self-administration. He states that when a fully responsible adult purchases a small amount of marijuana solely for personal use,

---

47 See also Hörnle, 'Der Schutz von Gefühlen', above n 39, 276–277.

48 This concept is very similar to the one developed by Joel Feinberg, which is based on the distinction between 'hard paternalism' and 'soft paternalism', with the latter allowing for state intervention only when the conduct concerned is 'substantially non-voluntary'. See Joel Feinberg, *Harm to Self* (Oxford University Press, New York 1986) 12 et seq. Also see Gerald Dworkin 'Paternalism', *The Stanford Encyclopedia of Philosophy* (Summer 2009 Edition), Edward N. Zalta (ed.) <http://plato.stanford.edu/archives/sum2009/entries/paternalism/>.

49 *Tötung auf Verlangen*, § 216 StGB: '(1) If a person is induced to kill by the express and earnest request of the victim the penalty shall be imprisonment from six months to five years. (2) The attempt shall be punishable.'

50 Of course, this view is not unchallenged. For different approaches see Thomas Gutmann, 'Der eigene Tod – Die Selbstbestimmung des Patienten und der Schutz des Lebens in ethischer und rechtlicher Dimension' (2002) *Ethik in der Medizin* 170; Arthur Kaufmann, 'Euthanasie – Selbsttötung – Tötung auf Verlangen' (1983) *Medizinrecht* 121. Also see Ronald Dworkin et al., 'Assisted Suicide: The Philosophers' Brief' (1997) 44(5) *The New York Review of Books* 41.

he or she does not harm anyone but perhaps themselves. Because of the lack of harm to a *Rechtsgut*, the criminalization can therefore be legitimately opposed.

A decision of the Federal Constitutional Court (*Bundesverfassungsgericht*),[51] which, by reference to the proportionality principle, ruled that in such cases the prosecutor or a court must abandon prosecution or at least punishment,[52] is a step in the right direction, but also produces legal uncertainty. Roxin states that it is unfortunate that the court did not adopt the *Rechtsgut* concept which would have provided a clearer solution.

Predominantly Symbolic Criminal Laws are to be Opposed While the previous edition of Roxin's text addressed this topic in only one short paragraph,[53] it is now expatiated on more than two pages. Symbolic criminal laws are laws which do not primarily protect legal goods/interests, but have a further, alternative function – namely, to allow the legislature to respond to topics currently prevailing in the public discourse.[54] Certain fears present in society may be laid to rest simply by passing the new law, even before its utility in preventing harm to a *Rechtsgut* has been proven.

This kind of legislation is called 'symbolic' because the enactment serves as a symbol for the state's capacity to take action against any social disturbance. As these symbols are 'condensation symbols' (in contrast to 'referential symbols')[55] they can be interpreted in different ways so that even totally different interests can be satisfied simultaneously.

Roxin uses a disputed offence to demonstrate the illegitimacy of predominantly symbolic criminal laws. In § 130(3) StGB, a particular form of incitement of the people is criminalized. The public approval, denial and/or belittlement of the international criminal law offences committed under the rule of the Nazis in Germany is punishable if this behaviour is capable of disturbing the public peace.[56]

51 BVerfGE 90, 145–226.

52 The abandonment of prosecution is regulated in §§ 153 et seq. of the Code of Criminal Procedure (*Strafprozessordnung* or StPO) and in § 31a BtMG. The abandonment of punishment is regulated in § 29(5) BtMG. Since these regulations generally give the prosecutor/court discretion as to whether prosecution or punishment is to be abandoned, the practice varies among different states.

53 Claus Roxin, *Strafrecht, Allgemeiner Teil, Band I: Grundlagen, Aufbau der Verbrechenslehre* (3rd edn C.H. Beck, Munich 1997) 19.

54 For details see Lauterwein, above n 29.

55 See Murray Jacob Edelman, *The Symbolic Uses of Politics* (University of Illinois Press, Urbana 1964) 6.

56 § 130(3) StGB reads: 'Whoever publicly or in a meeting approves of, denies or downplays an act committed under the rule of National Socialism of the type indicated in Section 6 subsection (1) of the Code of Crimes against International Law, in a manner capable of disturbing the public peace shall be punished with imprisonment for not more than five years or a fine.'

The Auschwitz Deception (*Auschwitzlüge*) is the most prominent example of such an offence.

While it is very hard to identify a good/interest protected by the offence, the symbolic effect is obvious:[57] Germany is depicted as a repentant country which neither forgets nor conceals the crimes committed by the Nazis. Despite the fact that, since the opposite is historically proven, anyone who approves, denies or belittles the crimes of the Nazis is either a fool or a liar, the simple stating of such an untruth does not affect the peaceful coexistence of the people. In contrast, the criminalization of such statements can be used to create a martyr and to support such a person's claim that the state uses the criminal law to suppress 'reality'.

Taboos are not Rechtsgüter The most famous example of a criminalized taboo is incest. Still an offence in Germany[58] – as well as in every Australian jurisdiction[59] – the protected *Rechtsgut* is not clear. The protection of the family unit, as often claimed,[60] cannot be the reason for criminalization since, on the one hand, an existing community of relatives is not a requirement for the offence and, on the other hand, persons who are members of a household but are not related by blood (for example stepfather and stepdaughter) cannot commit the offence, although sexual relationships between them do threaten the family unit.

Because in Germany only vaginal sex between close relatives is criminalized, one opinion argues that possible genetic defects would legitimate the offence. But this view ignores, first, that taking contraceptive measures does not provide a defence for the accused; secondly, that the chances of genetic defects actually occurring are not higher than for other at-risk groups (such as some people with intellectual disabilities or even women over a certain age); and thirdly, sexual conduct between members of these other at-risk groups, which might even have a much higher chance of conceiving a child with disabilities, is rightly not criminalized. The eugenics-based argument that a potential disability provides a reason to prohibit sexual conduct is an insult to persons with disabilities, as it implies that not being born at all is better than being born with a disability.

---

57 For details see Lauterwein, above n 29, 37–41.

58 § 173 StGB: '(1) Whoever completes an act of sexual intercourse with a consanguine descendant shall be punished with imprisonment for not more than three years or a fine. (2) Whoever completes an act of sexual intercourse with a consanguine relative in an ascending line shall be punished with imprisonment for not more than two years or a fine; this shall also apply if the relationship as a relative has ceased to exist. Consanguine siblings who complete an act of sexual intercourse with each other shall be similarly punished. (3) Descendants and siblings shall not be punished pursuant to this provision if they were not yet eighteen years of age at the time of the act.'

59 See Simon Bronitt and Bernadette McSherry, *Principles of Criminal Law* (2nd edn Thomson Lawbook, Pyrmont 2005) 604–605.

60 See also L. Waller and C.R. Williams, *Criminal Law: Texts and Cases* (10th edn LexisNexis Butterworths, Chatswood 2005) 126.

While the legislature did not follow the recommendations of the alternative draft of 1968 that proposed to decriminalize incest because of the lack of a legitimate *Rechtsgut*, the offence was recently challenged before the *Bundesverfassungsgericht*. The outcome of this case was much anticipated, as the court could have – for the first time – adopted the *Rechtsgutstheorie* in one of its judgements. The fact that the chair of the court's Second Senate, which dealt with the case, was – for the first time ever – a criminal law professor, Winfried Hassemer, who is furthermore one of the most prominent advocates of a very individual-focused *Rechtsgut* concept,[61] furthered this expectation. However, on 26 February 2008, the court ruled seven to one that the offence is constitutional.[62] Of the eight judges, only Hassemer wrote a dissenting opinion in which he argued that the offence was unconstitutional because none of its objectives were legitimate and, furthermore, the offence was not even capable of achieving these (illegitimate) goals.[63]

Objects of Protection that are too Abstract are not Rechtsgüter Roxin's final point concerns abstract terms, which must not be claimed as legal goods/interests. He gives two examples: first, the health of the nation (*Volksgesundheit*), which is often referred to as the protected *Rechtsgut* of the BtMG (Narcotics Act). The term health of the nation is fictive and only disguises the fact that, in reality, it concerns the protection of the health of many individual members of the nation. However, their health may only be protected by taking into consideration that deliberate self-harm and self-endangerment must not be criminalized. Therefore, the health of the nation does not provide for an additional reason for criminalization.

Secondly, the public peace (*öffentlicher Friede*) cannot be considered to be a *Rechtsgut* in itself.[64] All criminal offences (for example theft, assault, etc.) also protect the public peace – but only indirectly as they primarily protect other, much more concrete legal goods/interests (for example property, physical inviolability, etc.). How conduct could disturb public peace without impacting on peaceful coexistence as guaranteed by civil rights is not clear to Roxin. That some people might be upset by others expressing critical statements or extreme opinions cannot provide a reason for criminalization as such conduct is protected by civil rights.

No Nostrums but a Framework for Discussion After Roxin has presented the nine consequences of his theory, he comes to the conclusion that the *Rechtsgut*

---

61 His concept is called 'personal *Rechtsgut* concept' (*personaler Rechtsgutsbegriff*). See Hassemer, 'Darf es Straftaten geben', above n 1; Hassemer, *Theorie und Soziologie*, above n 26.

62 BVerfG, NJW 2008, 1137.

63 Hassemer combined tenets of the *Rechtsgutstheorie* with the concept of proportionality which the *Bundesverfassungsgericht* usually applies. See p. 94 et seq. for details.

64 See also Hörnle, 'Der Schutz von Gefühlen', above n 39, 271 et seq.

concept, which opponents consider unable to limit the criminal law, is indeed very capable of doing so if it is based on a social contract deduced from the objectives of criminal law and connected to constitutional rights.[65] He acknowledges that the concept does not provide nostrums for the problem of the legitimacy of criminal offences. But, he argues, it delivers concrete principles of reasoning which allow for a rational discussion of the state's power to criminalize conduct, and which can help to avoid the unconstitutional overexpansion of penal intervention.

The Expansion of the Criminal Law's Scope Beyond the Protection of Rechtsgüter

After this comprehensive and passionate defence of the *Rechtsgut* concept, the following section[66] in Roxin's text is, at first glance, confusing. It starts with the statement that 'obviously, exclusive limitation [of the criminal law] to the protection of *Rechtsgüter* does not completely do justice to the requirements of modern criminal law anymore'. This is due to developments in science, technology and industry which have created problems that a concept, which has its intellectual foundations in the Enlightenment, cannot solve. He gives three examples:

First, the protection of embryos poses questions that cannot be answered by the traditional concept of *Rechtsgüterschutz*. Since embryos are not yet human beings, the coexistence of already living humans is not directly affected by what can be done with embryos. On the other hand, since they are the precursor to human life, embryos cannot be denied entirely the protection of the criminal law. Where the line should be drawn is heavily disputed – legally, morally and medically. Roxin does not provide an answer, but states that neither of the radical solutions – no protection at all on the one hand and equality with the protection of humans on the other hand – is acceptable.

Secondly, the protection of animals and plants, and indeed creation per se, can become a function of the criminal law. This does not fit the traditional *Rechtsgut* concept. Roxin argues that many parts of creation are necessary conditions for safe human coexistence and therefore already fit within the concept. But, on the other hand, humans could still live together in peace and harmony if many endangered animals and plants became extinct. In former times this did not pose a problem because the destruction of vast areas of creation, as is possible today, was not imaginable. Roxin supposes that, being the 'masters of creation', humans should also bear responsibility for it. Therefore the state could use the criminal law to protect animals and plants, even if they are not of use for human social existence. Furthermore, since 2002, the German Constitution (*Grundgesetz* or GG) also provides that 'the state also protects animals'.[67]

65 Roxin, *Allgemeiner Teil, Band I,* above n 3, 29.

66 Ibid., 29–31.

67 Art. 20a GG: 'Mindful also of its responsibility toward future generations, the state shall protect the natural bases of life and the animals by legislation and, in accordance

Finally, Roxin sees the necessity of expanding the *Rechtsgut* concept to the lives of future generations. 'When we deplete the earth's resources, when we pollute the world because of our economic interests, deforest our woods and in the long run destroy our climate, this might not do harm to the current generation. But it deprives future generations of their basis of life.' A possible way to include future generations in the protection of legal goods/interests would be to expand the concept of the social contract to include them.[68] As with the protection of animals, the *Grundgesetz* today also states: 'Mindful also of its responsibility toward future generations, the state shall protect the natural bases of life.'[69]

Criminal Versus Administrative Offences

In this section,[70] Roxin discusses the *Rechtsgut* concept's inability to distinguish between criminal and administrative offences.[71] While in former times it was assumed that administrative offences did not protect *Rechtsgüter*, but merely ensured the enforcement of official orders (for example parking tickets or violation of compulsory registration), it is acknowledged today that both criminal and administrative offences protect *Rechtsgüter*. The reason for the existence of administrative offences is the principle of subsidiarity and the minor character of the harm to the protected *Rechtsgut* – but not its absence.[72]

---

with law and justice, by executive and judicial action, all within the framework of the constitutional order.' Roxin's reference to the responsibility of the 'masters of creation' appears to be unsystematic and challengeable. A concept more closely linked to the Constitution could avoid this problem by referring directly to Art. 20a GG.

68 See Roxin, *Allgemeiner Teil, Band I*, above n 3, 31.

69 Art. 20a GG.

70 Roxin, *Allgemeiner Teil, Band I*, above n 3, 31–32.

71 In German law, the distinction between criminal and administrative offences is very important. The Administrative Offences Act (*Gesetz über Ordnungswidrigkeiten* or OWiG) defines an administrative offence as 'unlawful and blameworthy conduct which fulfils the elements of a law that allows an administrative fine to be inflicted' (§ 1(1) OWiG). The most obvious difference to a criminal offence therefore lies in the possible legal consequences. While criminal offences can result in a fine or imprisonment (see §§ 38–43 StGB), an administrative offence can only result in an administrative fine. However, there are also many other differences concerning responsibility, procedure, etc. In contrast to Australia, the vast majority of public order offences and minor offences related to road safety and traffic are not criminal, but merely administrative offences.

72 The topic is further discussed in Roxin, *Allgemeiner Teil, Band I,* above n 3, 57–63.

The Mutability of the Rechtsgut Concept

The following section[73] of Roxin's work demonstrates that, despite its normative character, the *Rechtsgut* concept is not static but – within the framework of constitutional order – open to historical change and progress in empirical findings. Roxin uses the example of pornography. In Germany, the circulation of pornography among adults is not criminalized because, whatever one's moral judgement on the issue may be, its private consumption is considered to be socially harmless and can, it is argued, in some cases even contribute to the reduction of mental stress. However, if it were found that the consumption of pornography or specific types of pornographic material led to an increase in sexual offences, the *Rechtsgut* concept would not hinder criminalization.

Rechtsgut, Offences of Abstract Endangerment and Collective Rechtsgüter[74]

This section in Roxin's work[75] deals with some important issues, which can only be summarized here. First, Roxin states that the *Rechtsgut* concept does not require *actual harm* to a *Rechtsgut*. The *endangerment* of a *Rechtsgut* (*Rechtsgutsgefährdung*) is sufficient. Hence the criminalization of an attempt fits within the concept. Besides attempt, German criminal law acknowledges two different types of offences criminalizing the endangerment of a *Rechtsgut*: offences of concrete endangerment[76] and offences of abstract endangerment. While for the former, the actual occurrence of the danger to the *Rechtsgut* is an element of the offence,[77] in the latter, the protected *Rechtsgut* is not even identified in the offence, but only forms the basis or motive for criminalizing of the prohibited conduct.[78]

---

73 Ibid., 32–33.

74 *Rechtsgut, abstrakte Gefährdungsdelikte und Kollektivrechtsgüter.*

75 Roxin, *Allgemeiner Teil, Band I*, above n 3, 34–40.

76 *Konkrete Gefährdungsdelikte.*

77 For example § 315b(1) StGB, 'dangerous interference with road traffic' (*Gefährliche Eingriffe in den Straßenverkehr*), requires that a certain danger caused by the defendant's conduct, has actually occurred. § 315b(1) StGB reads: 'Whoever interferes with the safety of road traffic by: 1. destroying, damaging or removing facilities or vehicles; 2. setting up obstacles; or 3. undertaking a similar act of interference which is just as dangerous, and thereby endangers the life or limb of another human being or property of others of significant value, shall be punished with imprisonment for not more than five years or a fine.'

78 For example § 316 StGB, 'drunkenness in traffic' (*Trunkenheit im Verkehr*), only requires that the driver be too intoxicated to drive safely, not the occurrence of a dangerous incident. § 316 StGB reads: '(1) Whoever drives a vehicle in traffic (Sections 315 to 315d) although, due to consumption of alcoholic beverages or other intoxicants, he is not in a condition to drive the vehicle safely, shall be punished with imprisonment for not more than one year or a fine if the act is not punishable under Sections 315a or 315c. (2) Whoever commits the act negligently shall also be punished under subsection (1).'

Offences of concrete endangerment therefore fit well with the *Rechtsgut* concept, while the legitimacy of offences of abstract endangerment is in dispute.[79] The problem with these offences is seen in the 'shifting forward' of criminalization (*Vorverlagerung der Strafbarkeit*). In this manner, conduct which is still far from endangering a *Rechtsgut* could already be criminalized simply by reference to the general acceptance of this type of offences. Indeed, the number of offences based on abstract endangerment is increasing in German criminal law.

Another problem is caused by those offences that do not protect *Rechtsgüter* belonging to the individual, but only *Rechtsgüter* belonging to the collective (*Kollektivrechtsgüter* or *Universalrechtsgüter*). Some authors consider the *Rechtsgut* concept to be flawed in that it does not appear to be able to explain the existence of *Kollektivrechtsgüter*. But this is a misinterpretation. Even the most individual-focused version of the concept, the personal *Rechtsgut* concept, generally acknowledges the necessity of *Kollektivrechtsgüter*.[80] This version of the concept demands only that any legitimate *Rechtsgut* must serve the individual. However, it is easy to see that, for example, a functioning judicature, a stable currency and safe road traffic are necessary conditions for individuals' free self-determination, although they are *Rechtsgüter* belonging to the collective. The second problem related to *Kollektivrechtgüter* is related to the fact that a single offence generally does not affect the functionality of the *Rechtsgut*. For example, a single case of false testimony (or perjury) does not endanger the functioning of the judicature as a whole and one forged $50 note does not affect the stability of the currency. Nevertheless, the former *does* harm the administration of justice and the latter *does* harm the monetary system. And although the ecosystem of a lake might still function after someone illegally dumped toxic waste into it, it is still harmed. The scale of the harm inflicted is a question of subsidiarity, but it does not affect the general legitimacy of *Kollektivrechtsgüter*.

Without denying the general legitimacy of both *Kollektivrechtsgüter* and offences of abstract endangerment, Roxin argues that their combination can easily lead to the illegitimate criminalization of certain acts.[81] A good example of this is provided by the highly controversial offence of 'insurance abuse' (*Versicherungsmissbrauch*, § 265 StGB). While classic insurance fraud is punishable as fraud (*Betrug*, § 263 StGB[82]), the offence of insurance abuse criminalizes behaviour prior to the making of a false claim. Merely the act damaging of an insured object with intent to obtain insurance benefit is rendered

---

79 For details see Roxin, *Allgemeiner Teil, Band I*, above n 3, 35–37.

80 See Hassemer, 'Darf es Straftaten geben', above n 1.

81 Roxin, *Allgemeiner Teil, Band I*, above n 3, 38.

82 § 263(1) StGB reads: 'Whoever, with the intent of obtaining for himself or a third person an unlawful material benefit, damages the assets of another, by provoking or affirming a mistake by pretending that false facts exist or by distorting or suppressing true facts, shall be punished with imprisonment for not more than five years or a fine.'

criminal by § 265(1) StGB.[83] Further, § 265(2) StGB criminalizes even the attempt. The criminalization of such an early, preparatory, act could not be justified by reference to the property of the insurance company that may have had a claim filed against it at some future time. For this reason, attempts are being made to construct a *Kollektivrechtsgut* termed the 'efficiency of the insurance industry', which is, at this early stage, to be protected against abstract endangerment.[84]

The Protection of Rechtsgüter and the Constitution

The very important relationship between the *Rechtsgut* concept and the Constitution is examined in this section of Roxin's work.[85] As previously mentioned, the *Bundesverfassungsgericht* has not yet adopted the *Rechtsgut* concept. In contrast, in the recent decision on incest a majority of seven judges explicitly stated that criminal laws are not subject to any further, stricter standards as regards their objectives than those required by the Constitution itself. The *Rechtsgutstheorie* in particular was held not to apply to provide such further ongoing standards.[86] Therefore, with respect to any form of official act (being acts of legislation, administration and judication), the court applies the principle of proportionality as the crucial test for determining the legitimacy of criminal laws. The principle of proportionality consists of three elements: suitability, necessity and adequacy. As the court's breadth of interpretation of these criteria is very wide, the legislature's discretion is almost without limitation. The suitability of a law is rejected only if 'at the time of the enactment of the law, the enactment can be determined to be clearly ineffectual in achieving the goal'. The necessity of a law is denied only if there is another means available which would lead to the same result with less severe regulatory consequences. This is more a question of subsidiarity, for which, again, the legislature is given a wide scope for exercising discretion. Finally, the adequacy of a law is only denied if the action has to be determined to be 'plainly inadequate'. As the *Bundesverfassungsgericht* has held, '[i]n general, it is the legislature's business to determine the scope of criminal conduct.'[87]

While the academic community initially accepted the court's argumentation – most probably due to the fact that criminal law and constitutional law are traditionally considered to be two totally separate fields of scholarship – the

---

83 § 265 StGB reads: '(1) Whoever damages, destroys, impairs the usefulness of, gets rid of or gives to another a thing which is insured against destruction, damage, impairment of use, loss or theft, in order to obtain for insurance benefits himself or for a third party, shall be punished with imprisonment for not more than three years or a fine if the act is not punishable under Section 263. (2) An attempt shall be punishable.'

84 See Roxin, *Allgemeiner Teil, Band I*, above n 3, 38.

85 Ibid., 40–43.

86 BVerfG, NJW 2008, 1137, 1138, explicitly *contra* Roxin, *Allgemeiner Teil, Band I*, above n 3, 40–43.

87 BVerfGE 90, 173; BVerfG, NJW 2008, 1137, 1138.

court's approach has recently attracted strong criticism.[88] The criticism is based on the fact that the court regularly reviews the actions of the administration and the judicature, as well as those of the legislature, in fields other than criminal law, and with significant consequences. Meanwhile, in all areas, legislative acts rendering certain behaviours criminal are effectively unfettered by the constraints of constitutionality.

Nevertheless, the court did not adopt the *Rechtsgut* concept in its judgement on the possession of small amounts of marijuana, nor did it do so in the recent case on incest.

An Obligation to Criminalize?

A different question that arises from the *Rechtsgut* concept is whether the legislature can be *obliged* to criminalize certain conduct that harms or endangers a *Rechtsgut*.[89] Roxin is of the opinion that, in general, there cannot be such an obligation.[90] He argues that it is within the discretion of the legislature to consider the priority of individual freedom over collective welfare and to balance conflicting individual rights. The legislature also has the choice of several means to solve social problems, including the enactment of civil, administrative and criminal laws. On the other hand, there was one particular case in which the *Bundesverfassungsgericht* required the legislature to make use of the criminal law. In 1974, the offence of unlawful abortion was reformed and abortions within the first three months of a pregnancy were decriminalized. The law was challenged and the court declared it to be unconstitutional, reasoning that the legislature must not totally pass on the protection by the criminal law: 'In the most extreme case, when the protection demanded by the Constitution cannot be achieved by other means, the legislature can be obliged to apply criminal law in order to provide protection for a developing life.'[91] Roxin agrees in relation to this particular case where the destruction of such fundamental *Rechtsgüter* is at stake. However, under current law an abortion is

---

88 See, for example, Bernd Schünemann, 'Das Rechtsgüterschutzprinzip als Fluchtpunkt der verfassungsrechtlichen Grenzen der Straftatbestände und ihrer Interpretation' in Roland Hefendehl, Andrew von Hirsch and Wolfgang Wohlers (eds), *Die Rechtsgutstheorie: Legitimationsbasis des Strafrechts oder dogmatisches Glasperlenspiel?* (Nomos, Baden-Baden 2003) 133, 142 et seq.

89 Roxin, *Allgemeiner Teil, Band I*, above n 3, 43–44.

90 An exception is Art. 26(1) GG, which requires the legislature to criminalize acts that are intended to violate the peaceful coexistence of nations, especially the preparation of a war of aggression. Art. 26(1) GG reads: 'Acts tending to and undertaken with intent to disturb the peaceful relations between nations, especially to prepare for a war of aggression, shall be unconstitutional. They shall be made a criminal offence.'

91 BVerfGE 39, 1, 45.

not illegal[92] (except for other reasons,[93] for example medical grounds) if it is (1) conducted by a doctor, (2) professional abortion counselling has been obtained at least three days before the procedure, and (3) it is conducted within the first 12 weeks of a pregnancy.[94] The *Bundesverfassungsgericht* has also confirmed that the legislature may protect the unborn child by means other than criminalization.[95]

---

92 The criminal offence of an unlawful termination of pregnancy is stipulated in § 218 StGB: '(1) Whoever terminates a pregnancy shall be punished with imprisonment for not more than three years or a fine. Acts, the effects of which occur before the conclusion of the nesting of the fertilized egg in the uterus, shall not qualify as termination of pregnancy within the meaning of this law. (2) In especially serious cases the punishment shall be imprisonment from six months to five years. An especially serious case exists as a rule, if the perpetrator:

1. acts against the will of the pregnant woman; or
2. recklessly causes the danger of death or serious damage to the health of the pregnant woman. (3) If the act is committed by the pregnant woman, then the punishment shall be imprisonment for not more than one year or a fine. (4) An attempt shall be punishable. The pregnant woman shall not be punished for attempt.'

93 See § 218a(2)–(4) StGB: '(2) The termination of pregnancy performed by a physician with the consent of the pregnant woman shall not be unlawful, if, considering the present and future living conditions of the pregnant woman, the termination of the pregnancy is advisable to avert a danger to life or the danger of a grave impairment of the physical or emotional state of health of the pregnant woman and the danger cannot be averted in another way which is reasonable for her. (3) The prerequisites of subsection (2) shall also be deemed fulfilled with relation to a termination of pregnancy performed by a physician with the consent of the pregnant woman, if according to medical opinion an unlawful act has been committed against the pregnant woman under Sections 176 to 179 of the Criminal Code, strong reasons support the assumption that the pregnancy is based on the act, and not more than twelve weeks have elapsed since conception. (4) The pregnant woman shall not be punishable under Section 218a, if the termination of pregnancy was performed by a physician after counselling (Section 218) and not more than twenty-two weeks have elapsed since conception. The court may dispense with punishment under Section 218 if the pregnant woman was in exceptional distress at the time of the operation.'

94 § 218a(1) StGB: 'The elements of the offence under Section 218 shall not have been fulfilled, if:

1. the pregnant woman requested the termination of pregnancy and demonstrated to the physician with a certificate pursuant to Section 219 paragraph (2), sentence 2, that she had counselling at least three days before the operation; 2. the termination of pregnancy was performed by a physician; and 3. not more than twelve weeks had elapsed since conception.'

95 BVerfGE 88, 203.

The Subsidiarity of the Criminal Law

At the end of the description of his concept of *Rechtsgüterschutz*,[96] Roxin returns to its subsidiarity. The principle of subsidiarity is deduced from the principle of proportionality, which itself emanates from the rule of law (*Rechtsstaatsprinzip*). Being the most severe action by the state, the criminal law is considered to be the *ultima ratio*. The legislature must therefore consider other, less severe instruments (for example the law of torts or administrative offences) before invoking the criminal law.

Dissenting Opinions in the Literature

After Roxin establishes his concept, he presents the opinions of six different scholars who oppose the *Rechtsgut* concept.[97] The differing positions cannot be analysed in detail here, but they will be set out in the same manner as they are in Roxin's text. In this way, the manner in which German textbooks typically deal with dissenting opinions is also presented: they are mentioned and in many cases also analysed and argued against, but, obviously, not given the same attention as the position being argued.

Jescheck/Weigend,[98] *Zipf*[99]

These authors deny the concept's general capacity to solve problems relating to criminal legal policy. Nonetheless, some answers would be provided by the Constitution (for example the subsidiarity of the criminal law).

Welzel[100]

Welzel is of the opinion that the function of the criminal law is not the protection of legal goods/interests, but instead to secure the standing of positive social-ethical values, such as respect for other peoples' lives, health, freedom, property, etc. Its primary objective would be to safeguard the compliance with the values of legal attitude.

96 Roxin, *Allgemeiner Teil, Band I*, above n 3, 45–47.

97 Ibid., 47–52. This approach of presenting a view as well as dissenting opinions is typical for German law textbooks.

98 Hans-Heinrich Jescheck and Thomas Weigend, *Lehrbuch des Strafrechts: Allgemeiner Teil* (5th edn Duncker & Humblot, Berlin 1996) 257 et seq.

99 Heinz Zipf, *Kriminalpolitik: Ein Lehrbuch* (2nd edn C.F. Müller, Heidelberg 1980) 107 et seq.

100 Hans Welzel, *Das deutsche Strafrecht* (11th edn de Gruyter, Berlin 1969) 2 et seq.

Lenckner[101]

Lenckner supposes that a crime consists not only of the violation of a *Rechtsgut*, but also a breach of duty. Indeed, he argues, harm to a *Rechtsgut* is not even always necessary, whereas a breach of duty is. To illustrate this point he cites the punishability of an attempt which is doomed to failure. Obviously, this approach is only able to provide answers to the question why certain conduct *was* criminalized. Since the question – which duties may legitimately be protected by the criminal law – is not answered, the concept does not deliver normative statements on whether the criminalization is legitimate.

Jakobs[102]

For Jakobs, the main function of the criminal law is not the protection of *Rechtsgüter*, but the avoidance of damage to the standing of norms (*Verhinderung eines Normgeltungsschadens*). Punishment therefore means that the statement made by the offender (that the infringed norm is not valid) is not authoritative because enforcing the law demonstrates that the norm remains valid.[103] In contrast to the *Rechtsgut* concept, which is based on individual freedom and social contract theory, Jakobs' concept is based on social systems theory. Furthermore, Jakobs is one of the few scholars who avoid statements on the legitimacy or illegitimacy of the content of norms. He says that such statements are 'unscientific' and argues that they are a political and not scientific exercise.[104]

Amelung[105]

Amelung's material concept of crime refers to protection from anti-social behaviour (harm to society or *Sozialschaden*). Like Jakobs, his concept is based on social systems theory. In contrast to Jakobs, Amelung acknowledges that 'the reference to the system-functionality of conduct leads to the result that a person is not protected for his or her own sake but for the sake of society.' In order to avoid the final consequence that the individual could be sacrificed for the sake of society,

---

101 Adolf Schönke, Horst Schröder and Theodor Lenckner (eds), above n 3, 154.

102 Günter Jakobs, 'Was schützt das Strafrecht: Rechtsgüter oder Normgeltung?' in Takayuki Shiibashi (ed.), *Festschrift für Seiji Saito* (Tokyo 2003) 17–46.

103 This concept has obvious similarities to Hegel's retributive theory of punishment: punishment as the negation of the negation of the law.

104 The label 'political exercise' and the related objection to normative theories on the topic are characteristic of the Australian perspective. See Chapter 4 below for details.

105 Amelung, above n 4, 330 et seq. Also see Knut Amelung, 'Der Bergriff des Rechtsguts in der Lehre vom strafrechtlichen Rechtsgüterschutz' in Roland Hefendehl, Andrew von Hirsch and Wolfgang Wohlers (eds), *Die Rechtsgutstheorie: Legitimationsbasis des Strafrechts oder dogmatisches Glasperlenspiel?* (Nomos, Baden-Baden 2003) 155.

he limits his concept by adopting the fundamental values of the Constitution (especially human dignity and the right of personality). In this way, Amelung's approach offers similar results to Roxin's *Rechtsgut* concept. Roxin's critique states, of course, that Amelung's concept starts from the wrong end (society as being more important than the individual) and then, in order to produce the correct results, has to contradict its own foundation (by respecting individual dignity and freedom).

Stratenwerth[106]

As previously mentioned,[107] Stratenwerth is one of the best-known opponents of the *Rechtsgut* concept. He argues that the term *Rechtsgut* is too ambiguous. Furthermore, every group of people needs culturally determined norms of conduct which are not about goods/interests (*Güter*) at all. However, Stratenwerth also opposes the other concepts that are based on systems theory. They, in Stratenwerth's opinion, only produce highly abstract hypotheses and cannot deliver criteria critical to the definition of crime. He supposes that the criminal law is based on cultural codes of conduct which cannot be further explained by reason. He therefore considers the crucial fact to be whether conduct is socially and politically accepted or not wanted.

By simply asking if certain conduct is desired by the legislature or the majority of the population, Stratenwerth's concept surrenders the liberal basis of modern criminal law, which does not accept just any invasion of individual liberty by the parliamentary majority. When Stratenwerth argues that offences like incest, acts of exhibitionism or the already mentioned § 130(3) StGB[108] cannot be explained by the *Rechtsgut* concept, he ignores the fact that this is exactly the reason for doubting the legitimacy of these offences and is therefore not a weakness, but a strength of the concept.[109]

The Violation of a Subjective Right or an Interest

Dogmatically contiguous to the *Rechtsgutstheorie*, some authors replace the condition of harm or endangerment of a *Rechtsgut* with harm to a 'subjective right' or an 'interest'. These scholars do not object to the *Rechtsgut* concept in general, but rather present slight variations of the concept. Although Roxin does not explicitly

---

106 Günter Stratenwerth, 'Kriminalisierung bei Delikten gegen Kollektivrechtsgüter' in Roland Hefendehl, Andrew von Hirsch and Wolfgang Wohlers (eds), *Die Rechtsgutstheorie: Legitimationsbasis des Strafrechts oder dogmatisches Glasperlenspiel?* (Nomos, Baden-Baden 2003) 255; Stratenwerth and Kuhlen, above n 4.

107 Above n 4.

108 See above p. 14.

109 Roxin, *Allgemeiner Teil, Band I*, above n 3, 52.

deal with these approaches in his text, it is worthwhile mentioning them here because they illustrate some specific characteristics of the *Rechtsgutstheorie*.[110]

One approach replaces the criterion of harm or endangerment of a *Rechtsgut* as being the condition for criminalization with the necessity of the violation of a subjective right.[111] This opinion goes back to a concept developed by Feuerbach[112] and claims to be more liberal than the *Rechtsgut* concept.[113] Indeed, when originally raising the *Rechtsgut* concept against Feuerbach's concept of the violation of a right, Birnbaum[114] was also motivated by a desire to provide an explanation for the criminalization of incest, blasphemy and other moral offences which could hardly be argued to violate subjective rights.[115]

However, in terms of today's understanding this is not crucial since the modern *Rechtsgut* concept does not refer to Birnbaum's concept and the subsequent historical development, but refers instead to the concept of social contract theory and its idea of the possibility of free development of the individual, which the theory states should be safeguarded by the state.[116] According to this concept, moral and religious wrongs are not of harm to a *Rechtsgut*.

Therefore, both concepts point in the same direction, which is to limit the scope of the criminal law. However, in its modern version, the *Rechtsgut* concept detects the crucial minimum criterion for criminalization better than does the application of a criterion requiring a violation of a subjective right. Roxin argues that the question of whether a subjective right has been violated often does not help. The classic example to demonstrate this point is the debatable question of whether a subjective right exists that guarantees the undisturbed celebration of a funeral. However, Roxin insists that this is not a reasonable way to approach the problem. The legislator has to ask whether the safeguarding of dignified funeral celebrations is a condition for free and peaceful coexistence.

Furthermore, while the concept invoking a subjective right is questionably extendable on the one hand, on the other it is at the same time too narrow to comprise all conduct that is worthy of being punished. It has never been established which criteria are to be applied to determine subjective rights when dealing with collective *Rechtsgüter*. Offences of abstract endangerment also cannot be construed

110 These concepts are dealt with by Roxin in a forthcoming article: Claus Roxin, 'Zur neueren Entwicklung der Rechtsgutsdebatte' in *Festschrift für Winfried Hassemer* (forthcoming in 2010).

111 See, for example, Wolfgang Naucke, 'Schwerpunktverlagerungen im Strafrecht' (1993) *Kritische Vierteljahresschrift für Gesetzgebung und Rechtswissenschaft* 135, 137.

112 See Amelung, above n 4, 28 et seq.

113 See Gregor Stächelin, *Strafgesetzgebung im Verfassungsstaat* (Duncker & Humblodt, Berlin 1998) 45 et seq.

114 Birnbaum, above n 20.

115 See Amelung above n 4, 43 et seq; Schünemann, above n 88, 140.

116 Schünemann, above n 88, 141.

as being based on the violation of a subjective right. Of course, the supporters of this approach see this as being a great advantage of their concept.

In addition, the reference to subjective rights that always have existed does not provide for the possibility to react to changing circumstances. Yet, it cannot be doubted that the legislator has to be in a position to create new offences if changing circumstances throw up new possibilities of endangerment of peaceful human coexistence.[117]

Finally, the phenomenon of crime cannot be understood correctly if one regards it as being merely the violation of a right. The thief cannot destroy the right of the victim to his or her property because this right still exists despite the theft. The thief can, on the other hand, violate the actual authority to dispose of the stolen item, which is the actual *Rechtsgut* that is embodied in property. Similarly the murderer does not take the victim's right to live – but life itself.[118]

Similar statements can be made regarding the concept invoking a violation of an interest. This is particularly important with regard to the often-found English translation of *Rechtsgut* as a legal interest. As some German authors actually interpret the harm to a *Rechtsgut* as a violation of an interest, Roxin regards this concept as a version of the *Rechtsgut* concept.[119]

He sees the main problem with this approach in the fact that by simply referring to a legitimate interest one cannot identify which interest may be legitimate and the reasons why that may be the case. Interests are as different as are people. But the crucial feature of the *Rechtsgutstheorie* is the identification of what constitutes *legitimate* reasons for criminalization.

Furthermore, and similar to the approach invoking the violation of a subjective right, the violation of an interest is not a suitable criterion either because it is not the interest but the good that may be harmed.[120] If someone gets beaten, his or her interest in their bodily integrity persists. It is the bodily integrity itself that is affected.

Roxin argues that both the subjective right concept and the approach invoking the violation of an interest do not appreciate that the objects of protection in criminal law are in no way merely imaginary, but are in fact something real.

---

117 See Stächelin, above n 113, 46.

118 See Amelung, above n 4, 44.

119 Winfried Hassemer and Ulfried Neumann, 'Kommentierung zu § 1 StGB' in Urs Kindhäuser, Ulfrid Neumann and Hans-Ullrich Paeffgen (eds) *Strafgesetzbuch, Nomos-Kommentar* (2nd edn Nomos, Baden-Baden 2005) Vor § 1 m.n. 144.

120 See Roland Hefendehl, *Kollektive Rechtsgüter im Strafrecht* (Heymann, Cologne, Munich, Berlin 2002) 30.

Help from the English-speaking Debate?

After Roxin has laid down his own concept, discussed differing approaches and given further references to supporters and opponents of the *Rechtsgut* concept,[121] the next section[122] of his text deals with the harm principle.

This section did not exist in former editions of Roxin's text. In the new edition, Roxin expresses the view that efforts to limit the scope of criminal law by reference to the *Rechtsgut* concept are similar to the endeavours of Anglo-American scholars when referring to the harm principle. Although the term *Rechtsgut* is unknown in the Anglo-American debate, the harm principle as formulated by John Stuart Mill[123] would provide a similar function since it largely accords with the Enlightenment theory of social harm (*Sozialschadenslehre*).

Roxin then introduces Joel Feinberg's work[124] on the topic. While there are similarities to the *Rechtsgut* concept (no criminalization of merely moral wrongs and of self-harm), Feinberg's concept differs by introducing a second principle that legitimates criminalization: the 'offence principle'. Despite the differences in the structure (two legitimating principles instead of one), Roxin sees similarities in the content as the offence principle, too, provides that harassment that does not actually harm others should only be criminalized under qualified conditions.

Other authors have actually tried to enhance the German discussion by adopting the results of Feinberg's concept.[125] Seher, for example, argues that an approach like that of Feinberg, which acknowledges several principles rather than just one criterion in order to determine the legitimacy of an act of criminalization, would result in a more precise discussion than an approach like that of the *Rechtsgut* concept which insists on just one single criterion.[126] Seelmann, on the other hand, is of the opinion that both the *Rechtsgutstheorie* and the harm principle suffer from the same flaw: when it comes down to identifying the goods, interests, norms, etc.

121 Ibid., 53.

122 Ibid., 54–55.

123 John Stuart Mill, *On Liberty* (Penguin, London 1985, first published 1859).

124 Joel Feinberg, *The Moral Limits of the Criminal Law* (Oxford University Press, New York 1984–1988).

125 See Gerhard Seher, 'Prinzipiengestützte Strafnormlegitimation und der Rechtsgutbegriff' in Roland Hefendehl, Andrew von Hirsch and Wolfgang Wohlers (eds), *Die Rechstgutstheorie: Legitimationsbasis des Strafrechts oder dogmatisches Glasperlenspiel?* (Nomos, Baden-Baden 2003) 39; for another analysis of similarities and differences of the harm principle and the *Rechtsgutstheoriei*, see Kurt Seelmann, 'Rechtsgutskonzept, "Harm Principle" und Anerkennungsmodell als Strafwürdigkeitskriterien' in Roland Hefendehl, Andrew von Hirsch and Wolfgang Wohlers (eds), *Die Rechtsgutstheorie: Legitimationsbasis des Strafrechts oder dogmatisches Glasperlenspiel?* (Nomos, Baden-Baden 2003) 261; also see von Hirsch, above n 9. For a critical view on these attempts see Schönke, Schröder and Leckner (eds), above n 3, 153.

126 Seher, above n 125, 46.

that are to be protected by the criminal law, neither of the concepts could identify a plausible criterion that would justify criminalization.[127]

The section on the harm principle and the chapter on the *Rechtsgut* concept in Roxin's text conclude[128] with the statement that 'further elaboration of the *Rechtsgut* concept will have to consider the parallel Anglo-American developments for further discussion'.

Excursus: Additional Functions of the *Rechtsgut* Concept

As has already been stated, the *Rechtsgut* concept has – besides its function regarding criminal policy – further applications in German criminal law as it is considered to be a crucial factor in statutory interpretation. The term plays an important role especially with regard to defences.

This excursus will provide an introduction to the additional applications of the term *Rechtsgut*. While it is not intended to comprehensively present all its implications, the aim of this section is to demonstrate the general interdependence of the *Rechtsgut* concept and the German criminal law system and the way in which criminal law doctrine influences the application of the criminal law.

Statutory Interpretation

When interpreting a statutory criminal offence, one has to consider what *Rechtsgut* is protected by the prescription.[129] This is a special characteristic of the concept of teleological interpretation that is acknowledged by both academic lawyers and the courts. While teleological interpretation is an approach that is used in all fields of the law, the consideration of the protected *Rechtsgut* is only applicable in criminal law. Accordingly, every commentary on the Criminal Code will first present the *Rechtsgut* (or in some cases several *Rechtsgüter*) that is (or are) protected by a specific offence since this is regarded as being essential for the correct application of the law. However, because the individual offences do not always explicitly state which *Rechtsgut* they protect, the *Rechtsgut* itself has to be identified through

127 Seelmann, above n 125, 262.

128 There is actually one further section in the chapter. The last section deals with the 'criminal law for the enemy' (*Feindstrafrecht*), a concept developed by Jakobs which allows the legislature to treat 'enemies of state and society' differently to 'normal criminals'. The protective regulations in the substantive and the procedural criminal law should not apply to these 'non-persons'. As the concept was almost universally rejected and as it violates almost every constitutional right, it is not further discussed here. For details see Günther Jakobs, 'Bürgerstrafrecht und Feindstrafrecht' in Yu-hsiu Hsu (ed.), *Foundations and Limits of Criminal Law and Criminal Procedure – An Anthology in Memory of Professor Fu-Tsen Hung* (Teipei, 2003) 41.

129 Harro Otto, *Grundkurs Strafrecht, Allgemeine Strafrechtslehre* (7th edn De Gruyter, Berlin 2004) 8.

a process of interpretation.[130] For this reason, one often finds that the protected *Rechtsgut* of a particular offence is in dispute both among academics and between scholars and the courts.

When identifying the protected *Rechtsgut* of an offence one has to distinguish between the object of action (*Handlungsobjekt*) that is stated in the offence on the one hand and the protected *Rechtsgut* on the other.[131] Today it is acknowledged that there are three possible relationships between the two. First, both the object of action and the protected *Rechtsgut* can be identical, as is the case for fraud, where property is both the concrete object that is harmed by the offender and the *Rechtsgut* that is protected by the offence. Secondly, the object of action and the *Rechtsgut* can be identical with regard to content, but at the same time formally different. This is the case, for example, with manslaughter, where the object of action is a 'human', but the protected *Rechtsgut* is a human's 'life'. Finally, there can be a divergence between the two. That is, for example, true for theft, where the object of action is a particular item that does not belong to the thief while the protected *Rechtsgüter* are considered to be property and possession.

Although this approach to statutory interpretation has major consequences for a wide range of offences, only a few important examples will be provided here in order to illustrate the general implications.

Consent

The function of consent is not explicitly regulated in the German Criminal Code. Accordingly, there is a debate as to how consent is to be treated doctrinally. While some authors consider an act that is committed with the consent of the affected person (the 'victim') not to fulfil the elements of an offence,[132] the prevailing view in academic circles and amongst judges holds this to be true only for some offences. According to this opinion,[133] one has to distinguish between those offences that, due to their statutory wording, can only be committed against or at least in the absence of another person's will, such as criminal breach of trust,[134] which, under German law, requires a breach of duty by the offender. If the act is committed with the consent of the person to whom the duty is owed, it cannot be called a *breach*

130 See, for example, Harro Otto, *Grundkurs Strafrecht, Die einzelnen Delikte* (7th edn De Gruyter, Berlin 2005) 3.

131 See Roxin, above n 3, 33; Otto, above n 129, 8.

132 For example Roxin, above n 3, 544 et seq.

133 For example Wessels and Beulke, above n 3, 125 et seq.

134 § 266(1) StGB: 'Whoever abuses the power accorded him by statute, by commission of a public authority or legal transaction to dispose of assets of another or to obligate another, or violates the duty to safeguard the property interests of another incumbent upon him by reason of statute, commission of a public authority, legal transaction or fiduciary relationship, and thereby causes detriment to the person, whose property interests he was responsible for, shall be punished with imprisonment for not more than five years or a fine.'

of duty and therefore does not fulfil the elements of the offence. Further examples of such offences are theft[135] and unlawful entry.[136] With such offences, according to the prevailing opinion, the consent is called 'approval' (*Einverständnis*) in order to distinguish them from cases where consent is not considered to hinder the fulfilment of the elements of an offence, but only to provide a defence. Such offences are, for example, damage to property[137] and bodily harm.[138] In these cases, it is argued, consent does not change the nature of the act, which means that the property is still damaged and the body is still harmed. However, consent shall provide a defence for the accused.

While the distinction between the function of 'approval' and 'consent' seems to be scholastic at first glance, there are some crucial differences regarding the respective requirements. Valid consent, for example, requires a statement (verbally or by actions) which shows the will of the victim. For proper approval, on the other hand, the actual will of the victim is considered to be sufficient and it does not have to be articulated. Furthermore, mistake, deception and coercion are regarded as irrelevant to the question of approval, but instead to actually void consent. There are a few more differences, especially regarding the erroneous assumption of a proper approval or consent respectively.[139]

Now, with regard to the question of who is entitled to give both approval and consent, the *Rechtsgut* concept comes into play again. Only the bearer of a *Rechtsgut* is authorized to permit interference with one of his or her *Rechtsgüter*. While this may seem to be obvious, it has some crucial effects on which offences are subject to consent or approval in the first place. Taking commercial bribery[140] as an example, the importance of this interdependence between *Rechtsgut* and consent

---

135 § 242(1) StGB: 'Whoever takes moveable property not his own away from another with the intent of unlawfully appropriating the property for himself or a third person, shall be punished with imprisonment for not more than five years or a fine.'

136 § 123(1) StGB: 'Whoever unlawfully intrudes into the dwelling, business premises or other enclosed property of another, or into closed premises designated for public service or transportation, or whoever remains therein without authorization and does not leave when requested to do so by the authorized person, shall be punished with imprisonment for not more than a year or a fine.'

137 § 303(1) StGB: 'Whoever unlawfully damages or destroys the property of another shall be punished with imprisonment for not more than two years or a fine.'

138 § 223(1) StGB: 'Whoever physically maltreats or harms the health of another person, shall be punished with imprisonment for not more than five years or a fine.'

139 For details see Roxin, above n 3, 541–543.

140 § 299 StGB: '(1) Whoever, as an employee or agent of a business, demands, allows himself to be promised, or accepts a benefit for himself or another in a business transaction as consideration for giving a preference in an unfair manner to another in the competitive purchase of goods or commercial services, shall be punished by imprisonment for not more than three years or a fine. (2) Whoever, for competitive purposes, offers, promises or grants an employee or agent of a business a benefit for himself or for a third person in a business transaction as consideration, for his giving him or another a preference

becomes clear. This offence requires that an employee or an agent of a commercial operation receives a benefit for favouring the donor over his competitors with regard to the procurement of goods or commercial services for the operation. Although not undisputed, the prevailing opinion considers the integrity of free competition to be the protected *Rechtsgut* of the offence.[141] The property of competitors and the commercial operation are only regarded to be protected alongside this *Rechtsgut*. This leads to the result that the consent of the owner of the commercial operation does not hinder punishability of the employee or agent who accepts the benefit, because he or she is not the bearer of the *Rechtsgut* 'integrity of free competition'.[142] As with all *Kollektivrechtsgüter* the collective is the bearer of the *Rechtsgut* and therefore consent (or approval) is not possible for any of these offences (for example falsification of documents, road traffic offences).

If one were to consider the owner of the operation to be the bearer of the *Rechtsgut*, because the intention of the offence is to ensure that his or her personnel makes business decisions based on what is best for the company and not based on their own advantage, and therefore aims to protect the assets of the owner of the company, the owner's consent would, on the other hand, provide a defence for the accused. In this manner, the identification of the protected *Rechtsgut* by interpretation of a statutory offence determines the possibility of consent in the first place.

Another prime example of this interdependence is endangering road traffic.[143] This offence requires, among other things, that the driver of a vehicle endangers

---

in an unfair manner in the purchase of goods or commercial services, shall be similarly punished.'

141 Günter Heine, 'Commentary on § 299' in Adolf Schönke, Horst Schröder and Theodor Lenckner (eds), *Strafgesetzbuch: Kommentar* (27th edn C.H. Beck, Munich 2006), 2491.

142 Ibid., 2496.

143 § 315c(1) StGB:

'Whoever in road traffic:

1. drives a vehicle, although he: (a) due to consumption of alcoholic beverages or other intoxicants; or (b) due to mental or physical defects, is not in a condition to drive the vehicle safely; or
2. in gross violation of traffic regulations and recklessly: (a) does not observe the right-of-way; (b) improperly passes or drives improperly in the process of passing; (c) improperly drives over pedestrian crossings; (d) drives too fast in places with poor visibility, at road crossings or junctions or railroad crossings; (e) fails to keep to the right-hand side of the road at places with poor visibility; (f) turns, drives backwards or contrary to the direction of traffic, or attempts to do so, on a highway or motorway; or (g) fails to make vehicles which are stopped or have broken down recognizable for a sufficient distance, although it is required for traffic safety, and thereby endangers the life or limb of another human being or property of another of significant value,

shall be punished with imprisonment for not more than five years or a fine.'

the life or limb of another human being or property of another of significant value due to either not being in a condition to drive the vehicle safely (intoxication) or by grossly violating certain traffic regulations. Because the prevailing opinion and the courts consider general road traffic safety to be the protected *Rechtsgut* of the offence (a collective *Rechtsgut*), consent cannot constitute a defence.[144] According to another opinion, this result is illegitimate at least in one particular case, where the protected *Rechtsgut* is not general road traffic safety, but the individualized life and limb of a person. Therefore, the consent of a passenger, who knew of the driver's intoxication and his or her not being able to drive safely, but voluntarily took the chance of placing his or her own life at risk, should, according to this opinion, constitute a defence for the accused driver.[145]

Necessary Defence

In order to successfully invoke self-defence or defence of others, the accused must have acted in order to avert a current unlawful assault from himself/herself or someone else.[146] An assault is defined as the endangerment of a *Rechtsgut* by human conduct.[147] Because the assault has to be on the person invoking necessary defence or another person, only *Rechtsgüter* of the individual are subject to self-defence and defence of others, while averting attacks on collective *Rechtsgüter*, on the other hand, cannot be justified by invoking necessary defence.[148] Drunkenness in traffic,[149] for example, concerns the collective *Rechtsgut* 'road traffic safety' and can therefore not be lawfully prevented by someone invoking self-defence or defence of others. Cruelty to animals, too, is therefore not subject to self-defence or defence of others.[150]

---

144 Johannes Wessels and Michael Hettinger, Strafrecht, *Besonderer Teil 1, Straftaten gegen Persönlichkeits – und Gemeinschaftswerte* (32th edn C.F. Müller, Heidelberg 2008) 256.

145 See Peter Cramer and Detlev Sternberg-Lieben, 'Commentary on § 299' in Adolf Schönke, Horst Schröder and Theodor Lenckner (eds), *Strafgesetzbuch: Kommentar* (Criminal Code: Commentary) (27th edn C.H. Beck, Munich 2006), 2582–2583.

146 In German law, self-defence and defence of others are both dealt with under the topic *Notwehr*. § 32 StGB reads: '(1) Whoever commits an act, required as necessary defence, does not act unlawfully. (2) Necessary defence is the defence which is required to avert an imminent unlawful assault from oneself or another.'

147 Roxin, above n 3, 657.

148 Roxin, above n 3, 669 et seq.

149 § 316 StGB: 'Whoever drives a vehicle in traffic (Sections 315 to 315d) although, due to consumption of alcoholic beverages or other intoxicants, he is not in a condition to drive the vehicle safely, shall be punished with imprisonment for not more than one year or a fine if the act is not punishable under Sections 315a or 315c. (2) Whoever commits the act negligently shall also be punished under subsection (1).'

150 Necessity may provide a defence in such cases. However, necessity has different requirements than self-defence and does not allow for the same scope of actions.

Despite the term *Rechtsgut* not being stated in the statute regulating the defence, the first question one has to ask when considering whether an act is justified by necessary defence therefore is whether a 'self-defence-capable' or 'defence of others-capable' (*notwehrfähig*) *Rechtsgut* is concerned.

Necessity

In German law, the defence of necessity as justification[151] also requires the consideration of the affected *Rechtsgüter*. This is explicitly stated in § 34 StGB.[152]

First, there has to be an imminent danger to a *Rechtsgut*. Here, as with necessary defence, the endangered *Rechtsgut* itself does not have to be protected by the criminal law. A secure job, for example, has been considered by the courts to be a *Rechtsgut* that, when in imminent danger, can allow someone to invoke necessity, despite not being protected by the criminal law.[153] In contrast to necessary defence, collective *Rechtsgüter* are also considered to be protected by necessity.

Secondly, the endangered *Rechtsgut* needs to be weighed against the *Rechtsgut* that is affected by the act that is committed, so as to protect the former. Although not only the affected *Rechtsgüter*, but the entirety of all conflicting interests, have to be considered, the statute explicitly points out that the affected *Rechtsgüter* and the degree of danger threatening them are the most important aspects of these interests. The defence of necessity is only applicable if the protected interest (including the protected *Rechtsgut* and the degree of danger threatening it) substantially overweighs the one that was interfered with.[154]

---

151 Necessity can be a justification or an excuse in German criminal law. The former is regulated in § 34 StGB and the latter in § 35 StGB, and both have different requirements as well as consequences. Against an act that falls under necessity as an excuse, for example, another person is still entitled to use necessary defence measures because necessary defence only requires an *unlawful* assault and an act that is merely *excused* due to necessity is still unlawful. Necessity as justification, on the other hand, results in the act not being unlawful and therefore not being subject to necessary defence.

152 § 34 StGB reads: 'Whoever, faced with an imminent danger to life, limb, freedom, honour, property or another *Rechtsgut* which cannot otherwise be averted, commits an act to avert the danger from himself or another, does not act unlawfully, if, upon weighing the conflicting interests, in particular the affected *Rechtsgüter* and the degree of danger threatening them, the protected interest substantially outweighs the one interfered with. This shall apply, however, only to the extent that the act is a proportionate means to avert the danger.'

153 See Roxin, above n 3, 728–729.

154 Otherwise, necessity as excuse (§ 35 StGB) may be applicable: 'Whoever, faced with an imminent danger to life, limb or freedom which cannot otherwise be averted, commits an unlawful act to avert the danger from himself, a relative or person close to him, acts without guilt. This shall not apply to the extent that the perpetrator could be expected under the circumstances to assume the risk, in particular, because he himself caused the

This leads to the important result that, under German criminal law, the weighing of one life against another life can never result in necessity as justification. Accordingly, both the consideration of a 'more valuable' and a 'less valuable' life (for example, based on different life expectancies) as well as the comparison of the number of human lives affected (sacrifice one to save hundreds) are inadmissible.[155]

Attribution

Finally, another implication of the *Rechtsgut* concept concerns attribution.[156] The correlation of *Rechtsgut* and attribution is connected to the different structures of offences. The distinction between offences of concrete endangerment and offences of abstract endangerment on the one hand and between result crimes and conduct crimes on the other hand provides a good example. Generally, it is assumed that offences of concrete endangerment are also result crimes, while offences of abstract endangerment are conduct crimes.[157] The difference is important because only result crimes require causality and attribution regarding the action of the offender and the prohibited result. Mere conduct crimes, on the other hand, simply require a prohibited action by the offender. Accordingly, it is commonly argued, offences of abstract endangerment, since they do not require the occurrence of a prohibited result, are not subject to questions of causality and attribution. However, Schulenberg has pointed out that this was only true if one would wrongfully consider the protected *Rechtsgut* of an offence to be the criterion for the determination of whether an offence is a result crime or a conduct crime.[158] While it is correct, Schulenberg argues, to differentiate between offences of concrete endangerment and offences of abstract endangerment by asking whether or not there needs to be a concrete danger for the protected *Rechtsgut* in order to commit the offence, this,

---

danger or stood in a special legal relationship; however the punishment may be mitigated pursuant to Section 49 subsection (1), if the perpetrator was not required to assume the risk with respect to a special legal relationship. (2) If upon commission of the act the perpetrator mistakenly assumes that circumstances exist, which would excuse him under subsection (1), he will only be punished, if he could have avoided the mistake. The punishment shall be mitigated pursuant to Section 49 subsection (1).'

155 See Roxin, above n 3, 738–742.

156 See Johanna Schulenberg, 'Dogmatische Zusammenhänge von Rechtsgut, Deliktsstruktur und objektiver Zurechnung' in Roland Hefendehl, Andrew von Hirsch and Wolfgang Wohlers (eds), *Die Rechtsgutstheorie: Legitimationsbasis des Strafrechts oder dogmatisches Glasperlenspiel?* (Nomos, Baden-Baden 2003) 244 et seq.; Wolfgang Frisch, 'Rechtsgut, Recht, Deliktsstruktur und Zurechnung im Rahmen der Legitimation staatlichen Strafens' in Roland Hefendehl, Andrew von Hirsch and Wolfgang Wohlers (eds), *Die Rechstgutstheorie: Legitimationsbasis des Strafrechts oder dogmatisches Glasperlenspiel?* (Nomos, Baden-Baden 2003) 228 et seq.

157 See, for example, Roxin, above n 3, 421–432.

158 Schulenberg, above n 156, 247 et seq.

she insists, would not provide an answer to the question of whether the offence is a result crime or a conduct crime and, accordingly, whether causation and attribution need to be established. In order to distinguish between result crimes and conduct crimes, in Schulenberg's opinion, one must not consider whether there needs to be a concrete endangerment to the protected *Rechtsgut*, but one has to consider whether there needs to be the occurrence of a result regarding the *concrete object of action*. She uses the offence of negligent arson (§ 306d(1) StGB in conjunction with § 306(1) Nr. 1 StGB) as an example.[159] This offence is generally considered to be an offence of abstract endangerment with the protected *Rechtsgüter* being the life and limb of the dwellers. Accordingly, the offence does not require a concrete danger to the life and limb of people. However, Schulenberg argues, it still requires the determination of causation and attribution – not with respect to the endangerment of the protected *Rechtsgüter*, but regarding the concrete object of action; in this case, the building, ship, hut or other premises which serves as a dwelling for human beings. Only if the catching of fire was caused and can be objectively attributed to an act of the accused can he or she be guilty of the offence. With respect to negligence, this leads to the result that in cases where a person only caused a permitted risk (for example, indoor welding in compliance with all regulations), which lead to a dwelling catching fire, he or she is not punishable for negligent arson because the fire cannot be attributed to the person's actions since they were within the permitted risk.[160]

Methodological Interdependence

As this excursus has shown, the *Rechtsgut* concept has several methodological implications regarding the application of the criminal law. Despite the fact that these implications do not directly concern crime policy questions, the interdependence of statutory interpretation and the *Rechtsgut* concept on the one hand and the crime policy function of the concept on the other hand automatically results in an interaction of crime policy and the criminal law system.[161]

---

159 § 306d(1) StGB reads: 'Whoever acts negligently in cases under Sections 306 subsection (1), or 306a subsection (1), or negligently causes the danger in cases under Section 306a subsection (2), shall be punished with imprisonment for not more than five years.'

§ 306a(1) StGB reads: 'Whoever sets fire to, or, as a result of setting a fire, or destroys, in whole or in part: 1. a building, ship, hut or other premises which serves as a dwelling of human beings; 2. a church or another building which serves for the practice of religion; 3. a premises which serves temporarily as a residence for human beings at a time in which human beings usually reside there, shall be punished with imprisonment for not less that one year.'

160 For details on attribution and permitted risk see Roxin, above n 3, 382–384.

161 For details on this relationship see Roxin, 'Crime Policy and the Criminal Law System', above n 13.

Accordingly, the two functions of the *Rechtsgut* concept – the methodological and the critical one – do not exist independently of each other, but, as long as the *Rechtsgut* concept is regarded as fulfilling a critical function concerning criminal policy, the methodological function too will always be influenced by this. The most obvious example of this interdependence is provided by the methodologically crucial question of which *Rechtsgut* is protected by a certain offence. The answer to this question will always be dependent on which *Rechtsgüter* one generally considers to be a legitimate subject to be addressed by criminalization. In this manner the everyday application of the criminal law is influenced by the *Rechtsgut* concept and the debate on legitimate limits of the criminal law – independently of whether or not this is actually realized by practising lawyers.

A Dogmatic Tool for Critique

As seen, in German criminal law theory the limits of criminal law are deduced from its general function. The leading doctrine describes this function to be the protection of legal goods/interests (*Rechtsgüterschutz*) and argues that any behaviour which does not endanger a *Rechtsgut* may not be criminalized. As the discussion of Roxin's concept as an example has shown, the theory is (besides its undisputed methodological implications for statutory interpretation) a dogmatic attempt to limit the legislature's discretion when criminalizing conduct. Further, although the concept itself is well established in Germany, the definition of the term *Rechtsgut* is heavily disputed. Discussions on whether a certain form of behaviour is legitimately criminalized are held within the framework of the concept, and different definitions are suggested for the term *Rechtsgut*. In this way, the theory only provides a common basis and guide for the discussion – it does not deliver uniform answers. Issues like the protection of animals and the environment, the legitimacy of *Kollektivrechtsgüter* and offences of abstract endangerment, as well as new problems such as the protection of embryos, challenge the concept's ability to provide clear answers. But, despite the difficulties the concept faces and, due to that, the necessary alterations to the theory, the *Rechtsgutstheorie* is still regarded to be 'the essential basis for a rational criminal law system' by the vast majority of German criminal law scholars.[162]

The *Rechtsgutstheorie* is an academic invention. It was developed by scholars and is discussed and enhanced in academic writings, presented in criminal law texts and taught at universities. Through the publication of the alternative drafts, it also influenced legislative reform work in the 1960s and has been used to influence and critique legislative decisions since then. It has, on the other hand, not been adopted by the Federal Constitutional Court, which determines the legitimate scope of the criminal law – as with any other field of the law – by applying the concept of proportionality.

162 See von Hirsch, above n 9.

In summary, the *Rechtsgutstheorie* provides the basis for academic critique of the legislative practice in German criminal law. The fact that the Constitutional Court does not apply the theory is disappointing to its supporters, but is not considered to be a flaw in the theory nor to decrease its value. In contrast, the recent judgement on incest has provoked critical responses by academics and practising lawyers.[163] In this manner, the *Rechtsgutstheorie* was not weakened by the judgement, but the judgement is being criticized by use of the theory. The dissenting opinion of Hassemer provides strong support for this criticism as it shows how the practical application of the theory can be managed by the court without surrendering its classic criteria – the concept of proportionality – but by combining it with the claims of the *Rechtsgutstheorie*.[164]

This relationship between law in practice, as articulated in the judgements of courts, and law in theory, as formulated by legal scholars, is a fundamental part of legal culture and legal education in Germany. Further, it is not a static but a productive relationship as both worlds influence each other: sometimes the courts adopt theories developed by scholars and sometimes the academic lawyers agree with the principles developed by the courts. It is important to realize, however, that legal education at German universities, and, accordingly, the style of German law textbooks, reflects this system: students are not supposed to learn a single solution to a legal problem (neither the courts' nor an academic's opinion). They are taught to recognize the many different solutions available and to argue for and against them. Which opinion the students finally adopt is irrelevant – as long as they have presented and discussed the different possibilities and justified their position with reasonable arguments.[165] This is true not only for questions of statutory interpretation, but also, even more, for general questions about legal

163 Tatjana Hörnle, *Inzest-Urteil – 'Das Verbot ist nicht plausibel' – Spiegel-Interview mit Professorin Tatjana Hörnle* (15 March 2008) Spiegel Online <http://www.spiegel.de/panorama/justiz/0,1518,541628,00.html> accessed 19 June 2009; Tatjana Hörnle, 'Das Verbot des Geschwisterinzests – Verfassungsgerichtliche Bestätigung und verfassungsrechtliche Kritik' (2008) *NJW* 2085; Friedhelm Hufen and Matthias Jahn, 'Anmerkung zu BVerfG, NJW 2008, 1137' (2008) *JuS* 550; Benno Zabel, 'Die Grenzen des Tabuschutzes im Strafrecht' (2008) *JR* 453; Jörg Ziethen, 'Anmerkung zu BVerfG, NJW 2008, 1137' (2008) *NStZ* 617.

164 The *Rechtsgutstheorie* only demands that every criminal offence must have a legitimate goal – the protection of a *Rechtsgut* – and tries to establish rules to determine legitimate *Rechtsgüter*. The concept of proportionality, on the other hand, already requires a legitimate goal for its application. While the *Rechtsgutstheorie* is used to determine the legitimacy of legislative goals, the concept of proportionality is used to detect whether the means to achieve these (legitimate) goals are proportionate and therefore legitimate.

165 While this is true for legal education at German universities and the final exam (the First State Exam), the situation is different in the Second State Exam, which is taken after a two-year clerkship and entitles the successful candidate to work as a legal practitioner (attorney, prosecutor, judge, public notary, etc.). As the clerkship and the Second State Exam are totally separate from the universities and governed entirely by the States' Departments

theory. As long as the argumentation is embedded in the established structure of the *Rechtsgutstheorie*, the definition of the term *Rechtsgut* which a lawyer (or student) chooses to apply is not decisive for the legitimacy of the argument. And even if one were to argue against the *Rechtsgut* concept, this would not be seen as being doomed to failure, but would also require a sound knowledge of the concept in order to dogmatically challenge it.

---

of Justice, the candidates are supposed to apply the courts' decisions instead of scholarly opinions wherever possible.

Chapter 3
The Approach to the Problem – A Problem Itself

> The reason that I am expressing reluctance to engage in that kind of intellectual exercise is because it is foreign to the way that this legal culture approaches law. What you have described is a kind of a top-down type process of developing the law; a global theory, which is then applied to the practical world. The legal culture of this country, as indeed most legal systems which have origins in the English legal model, is a much more pragmatic, ad-hoc type of culture where the law develops on a case by case basis. And the common law, that is the law that is made by the judges, is not the result of any coherent theory but a long historical development whereby individual judges are trying to do what seems to be just in individual cases. The law develops in that way through millions of accretions to a particular point where you can say, this is the legal position.[1]

The Original Plan and its Alteration

As we have seen, the *Rechtsgutstheorie* faces new challenges. Following from this, not only Roxin but also other (German and English) scholars recently discovered the Anglo-American discussion as a potential source for further development of the concept.[2] Taking these attempts into consideration, the original aim of this analysis was to analyse the Australian understanding of the *function* (or the *purpose*) of criminal law and to investigate if criminal legislation in Australia confirms this understanding. Australia, in contrast to the United Kingdom and the United States, had not been included in the investigations of the discussions in English-speaking countries referred to above.

---

1 Interview with Stephen Odgers (Sydney, 27 August 2007).

2 See Gerhard Seher, 'Prinzipiengestützte Strafnormlegitimation und der Rechtsgutbegriff' in Roland Hefendehl, Andrew von Hirsch and Wolfgang Wohlers (eds), *Die Rechstgutstheorie: Legitimationsbasis des Strafrechts oder dogmatisches Glasperlenspiel?* (Nomos, Baden-Baden 2003) 39; Kurt Seelmann, 'Rechtsgutskonzept, "Harm Principle" und Anerkennungsmodell als Strafwürdigkeitskriterien' in Roland Hefendehl, Andrew von Hirsch and Wolfgang Wohlers (eds), *Die Rechtsgutstheorie: Legitimationsbasis des Strafrechts oder dogmatisches Glasperlenspiel?* (Nomos, Baden-Baden 2003) 261; also see Andrew von Hirsch, 'Der Rechtsgutsbegriff und das "Harm Principle"' in Roland Hefendehl, Andrew von Hirsch and Wolfgang Wohlers (eds), *Die Rechtsgutstheorie: Legitimationsbasis des Strafrechts oder dogmatisches Glasperlenspiel?* (Nomos, Baden-Baden 2003) 13.

The original intention was therefore to analyse the Australian understanding of the function of criminal law in order to gain new perspectives for the German discussion. The idea was that in Australia, a country with a common law tradition but in which the criminal law has been partly codified, there was likely to be an extensive academic discussion on the purpose of criminal law. The original aim was to analyse this discussion and the legislative practice.

But, after commencing the Australian research, it soon became clear that this project was not as easy to carry out as expected. The mistake was the assumption that the Australian discussion is similar to the German. The reality is that it is fundamentally different.

First of all, in contrast to Germany, there is no one leading doctrine on the *function* (or the *purpose*) of criminal law established in Australia. In Germany, it is commonly assumed that the leading doctrine in English-speaking criminal law theory is based on the harm principle as it was established by J.S. Mill[3] and further developed by Joel Feinberg.[4] It is therefore also often assumed that the harm principle is the equivalent of the *Rechtsgutstheorie*.[5] This is not the case, at least in Australia where the harm principle has nowhere near the level of influence that the *Rechtsgutstheorie* has in Germany. As far as could be established, there is not one single piece of Australian academic writing that argues that the *only* purpose of the criminal law is the prevention of harm to others and that therefore *only* such conduct as is (potentially) harmful should be criminalized.

Secondly, Australian literature on the legitimate scope of the criminal law is very scarce. In contrast to Germany, many Australian criminal law texts do not deal with questions surrounding this topic. Only a few, newer textbooks include such a discussion, while monographs or journal articles on the topic generally (and not in context of a particular offence) apparently do not exist.[6] This is probably the most prominent difference compared to Germany, where extensive academic discussion of the general topic is articulated in textbooks, commentaries, monographs and journal articles.

Thirdly, the method of deducing the limits of criminal law from its purpose, as it is characteristic for the *Rechtsgutstheorie*, does not seem to be applied in Australian criminal legal scholarship. Nor do Australian scholars attempt to establish a normative theory on the *limits* of criminal law which is independent

---

3 John Stuart Mill, *On Liberty* (Penguin, London 1985, first published 1859).

4 Joel Feinberg, *Harm to Others* (Oxford University Press, New York 1984).

5 See Marco Mansdörfer (ed.), *Die allgemeine Straftatlehre des Common Law: Eine Darstellung unter besonderer Berücksichtigung des englischen Strafrechts* (C.F. Müller, Heidelberg 2005) 1–10; Claus Roxin, *Strafrecht, Allgemeiner Teil, Band I: Grundlagen, Aufbau der Verbrechenslehre* (4th edn C.H. Beck, Munich 2006) 54–55.

6 See, for example, David Brown et al., *Brown, Farrier, Neal and Weisbrot's Criminal Laws: Materials and Commentary on Criminal Law and Process of New South Wales* (4th edn Federation Press, Leichhardt 2006) Chapter 2; Simon Bronitt and Bernadette McSherry, *Principles of Criminal Law* (2nd edn Thomson Lawbook, Pyrmont 2005) Chapter 1.

of the *purpose* of criminal law. Instead, Australian scholars – if they deal with the problem at all – refer to *several* independent principles in order to discuss the limits of the criminal law.[7] Furthermore, the principles referred to were not developed by Australian scholars, but were formulated in the United Kingdom or the United States. Australian academics also appear not to critique or enhance these principles, but simply refer to them.[8] A comprehensive discussion on these limiting principles is lacking in Australian academic writing.

Finally, in contrast to Germany, where the criminal law reform of the 1960s attracted vast academic discussion which had crucial influence on the reforms,[9] Australian scholars have been criticized for not even trying to influence a recent codification project concerning the criminal law.[10]

If one finds the kind of discussion referred to here in Australia at all, then it is generally related only to specific contexts such as drug laws or Indigenous crime; it is not developed as a general normative theory of the function, purpose, aims or limits of criminal law.

Although recent attempts to combine the Anglo-American ideas with the German theory seem promising, they often seem to suffer from the mistake described above in that they do not consider the fundamental differences of the two approaches.

As the harm principle is not a single Anglo-American doctrine used to describe the function of criminal law, but just one of several principles to describe its limits, it cannot be simply placed at the same level as the *Rechtsgutstheorie*. Furthermore, it is not useful to attempt to incorporate the Anglo-American approach into the German theory simply by referring to Joel Feinberg's work from the 1980s without analysing the current opinion in the English-speaking discussion. For this reason recent attempts to combine the two approaches lack a sufficient analysis of the English-speaking perspective.

Thus, this book focuses on an analysis of the Australian understanding of the limits of criminal law and compares the results with the *Rechtsgutstheorie* in order to demonstrate the fundamental differences as well as existing similarities.

An Analysis Using Contextual and Comparative Elements

Having defined the scope of the analysis, the question of how this task could reasonably be conducted arises. As already mentioned, the discussion in the Australian literature is not extensive and there is no leading doctrine established to describe the limits of criminal law. But the lack of a comparable *doctrine* is

---

7 See Bronitt and McSherry, above n 6, 52–68.

8 See Brown et al., above n 6, 12.

9 See Roxin, *Allgemeiner Teil, Band I*, above n 5, 116–118.

10 See M.R. Goode, 'Constructing Criminal Law Reform and the Model Criminal Code' (2002) 26 *Criminal Law Journal* 152, 157.

not a compelling argument against such a comparison, because the *problems* that the *Rechtsgutstheorie* deals with also exist in Australia.[11] One of the fundamental conclusions of the German theory is that merely moral wrongs do not affect a *Rechtsgut* and therefore must not be criminalized.[12] In Australia, a discussion about the criminalization of moral wrongs also takes place; it is just not embedded within a general theory. The same can be said about the criminalization of merely offensive conduct and self-harm.

It appears that the principles referred to by Australian scholars are intended to deal with the same problems as the *Rechtsgutstheorie* does. The approach, however, is totally different as the German theory only accepts one reason for criminalization, which is deduced from the function of the criminal law, while Australian scholars invoke several, independent principles.

Despite the lack of comparable doctrines, it is therefore still possible to compare the different approaches to attempts to solve the same problems in both countries. Nevertheless, this still does not resolve how the comparison could be conducted in terms of methodology. The problem is that neither the conventional approach to legal comparison, which simply asks 'How do they do it here and how do they do it there?', nor a comparative contextual analysis[13] perfectly suits the purpose of this book. For classic legal comparison, the well-elaborated concept on the one hand and the lack of a discussion on the other hand pose an insuperable obstacle. It would be a fairly useless exercise as it would simply tell us that while in Germany the *Rechtsgutstheorie* is applied, no similar theory is used in Australia. On the other hand, a comparative contextual analysis, which 'requires an appreciation of the social reality of historical, social, political, and economic variables',[14] would investigate and compare reasons for the differences between the countries. However for the purposes of this book, which is an analysis of the Australian perspective, the fundamental difference between the two countries with regard to the level of discussion on the topic also poses a problem for this method. While it is intended that the social, historical, etc. reasons for the situation in Australia be analysed, a comparison of these influences with those on the German theory is not planned. For the purposes of this book, the *Rechtsgutstheorie* will only provide a

11 For the general benefits of an approach focusing on common problems rather than on comparing different doctrines, see Geoffrey Wilson, 'Comparative Legal Scholarship' in Mike McConville and Wing Hong Chui (eds), *Research Methods for Law, Research Methods for the Arts and Humanities* (Edinburgh University Press, Edinburgh 2007) 87, 92–94. It is important to realize however that Wilson's suggestions concern the comparison of *legal systems*, while this book compares concepts of *legal theory*.

12 See above p. 11.

13 For the advantages of comparative contextual analysis, see Mark Findlay and Ralph Henham, 'Integrating Theory and Method in the Comparative Contextual Analysis of Trial Process' in Mike McConville and Wing Hong Chui (eds), *Research Methods for Law, Research Methods for the Arts and Humanities* (Edinburgh University Press, Edinburgh 2007) 104.

14 Ibid.

model for the analysis of the Australian discussion; it provides an example for an elaborated concept used to approach the problem. In other words, a comparative contextual analysis would compare the contextual reasons for both the Australian and the German approaches to dealing with the problem. However, this is not the purpose of this book, which aims only to analyse the Australian perspective and uses the *Rechtsgutstheorie* as an example for a possible, totally different, approach to dealing with the same question.

Therefore, while the contextual level has played some role in the description of the *Rechtsgutstheorie* in Chapter 2, it will further play a crucial part in the analysis of the Australian understanding. It is important to ask what sociocultural reasons have influenced the way the question is approached (or neglected) in Australia. Thus, the analysis of the discussion in Australia will make reference to historical, constitutional and cultural contexts, but the book as a whole will not apply the methodology of comparative contextual analysis. Hence, the methodology applied can be termed 'an analysis using contextual and comparative elements'.

The Lack of Literature: Time for a Talk

Having narrowed both the scope and the methodology of the analysis, the major problem is still not resolved; the lack of academic writing on the limits of criminal law in Australia is, obviously, an obstacle for an analysis of this topic.

In order to increase the number of sources for the investigation, it was therefore necessary to leave the familiar terrain of literature analysis. The fact that there was not much academic literature on the topic available could, looked at from a different perspective, even be beneficial for the analysis. Just because few scholars have written on the topic need not necessarily mean they do not have thoughts on it. And perhaps these thoughts could even provide an additional reason for the lack of literature. For this reason it was necessary to include an empirical aspect to the research. It was time to seek more information by talking to Australian experts who deal with questions of criminal law – either as academics, practitioners or law reformers. Additionally, besides asking about the limits of criminal law, the experts might also give valuable testimonies on the reasons for the topic having been neglected in the Australian literature.

Taking into consideration the fact that a mere literature analysis could not have answered both questions, one is certainly justified in concluding that, despite being born of necessity, the empirical part actually enhances the analysis.

The Questions

The interviews with the Australian experts were intended to provide answers to three different sets of questions:

1. What principles may legitimately limit the scope of criminal law?
2. Why is there no comprehensive discussion on this topic in the Australian academic writing?
3. Are certain individual offences that are considered illegitimate in terms of the German *Rechtsgutstheorie* also controversial in the Australian arena?

Accordingly, the interviews were divided into three parts:

1. General questions on limiting principles in the criminal law (four questions).
2. Questions on the sources of knowledge in this area (two questions).
3. Questions concerning the legitimacy of individual offences (four questions).

Finally, there was an additional question concerning the theory of Joel Feinberg.[15]

Because the interviews were to provide further, qualitative sources for the analysis of the Australian understanding of the topic, they were conducted as semi-structured expert interviews.[16] While all experts were asked the same 11 questions in the same order, all of the questions were open-ended so that the interviewees were given opportunity to provide individual in-depth answers based on their personal experience, education and opinion.

The Interviewees

The challenge of choosing the experts to participate in interviews was not as difficult as expected, considering the great number of law schools in Australia. In Germany, just listing all the academics dealing with criminal law theory would probably be a day's work. Interestingly, the list of potential interviewees was quite short. This is due to the fact that, despite the numerous law schools in Australia, the number of scholars who are interested in and deal with the questions relevant to this analysis is quite small.

In addition to academics who focus on criminal law, it was also decided to include experts working as practitioners in criminal law (as judges, solicitors,

15 For a list of the questions asked see Appendix A, p. 137.

16 See Andrea Fontana and James H. Frey, 'The Interview: From Structured Questions to Negotiated Text' in Norman K. Denzin and Yvonna S. Lincoln (eds), *The Handbook of Qualitative Research* (2nd edn Sage, Thousand Oaks 2000) 645, 649–656.

barristers or public prosecutors) as well as lawyers who deal with law reform issues (through law reform commissions or Attorney Generals' departments). The reason for this is the fact that it is understood that the Australian discussion does not necessarily take place only in academic writing and therefore the search for information should not be restricted to academics. In other words, perhaps the fact that there is not much academic writing on the topic is due to a difference in the 'sourcing of knowledge' between Australia and Germany. Perhaps the Australian practitioners – especially the judges – would have even more to say about the topic than the academics. And, as the institution of law reform commissions plays an eminent role in Australia,[17] it would be negligent to exclude them from the survey as well.

The final list of interviewees contained 17 experts in criminal law, who were either academics, practitioners, law reformers or a combination of these. After initial contact was made with all of the experts, several were fairly eager to participate, while others, at first, did not respond at all. Finally, interviews were conducted with 11 experts:[18] two (current or former) judges of the High Court of Australia; six (current or former) academics; two law reform workers; two practitioners (a barrister and a solicitor) in the field of criminal law; and a Director of Public Prosecutions.

For the purposes of this analysis, it was not important that the interviewees not know what questions they were going to be asked before the actual interview and, therefore, they were given information on the content of the interview in advance. Therefore, they knew what to expect and could prepare themselves for the interview if they wished.

The Interviews

Each interview was conducted at the interviewee's office and audio-recorded. The interviewees were informed that they would be provided with a transcript of their interview and that none of their statements would be used until they had approved the transcripts. As mentioned before, the purpose of the interviews was not to gain spontaneous answers, but to obtain further, well-reasoned information on the topic. The participants were therefore encouraged to edit their transcripts if they wanted to alter any of their statements.

Although all of the interviewees were asked each of the 11 prepared questions, the duration of the interviews varied considerably. While the shortest interview was finished in 30 minutes, the longest took over 70 minutes. Most of the interviewees were well prepared for the questions (some of them even said they had looked at relevant literature in preparation for the interview). However, a couple of

17 See, for example, the nearly 1,000-page report of the Australian Law Reform Commission, *Same Crime, Same Time: Sentencing of Federal Offenders, Report 103* (ALRC, Sydney 2006).

18 For a list of the interviewees see Appendix B, p. 139.

participants (who were practitioners) were observably uncomfortable with the whole topic as they considered it not to be within their field of expertise.

All of the interviews were conducted in the same manner: the interviewees were asked a question and given as much time as they needed to answer. All the questions were asked in the same order and, except for a few exceptions, the interviewees themselves did not have any questions or difficulty understanding what they were being asked about. In the rare cases where an interviewee did not understand the question perfectly, it was explained until the topic was clear. At times it was necessary to come back to a question because the expert had wandered too far from the topic.

The Results

All the interviewed experts eventually approved their transcripts. While some did not make any changes at all, others altered almost every one of their statements. Some of the transcripts were approved within a few days of the interview, while two of the interviewees did not approve their statements until seven months after the interviews took place.

Combined, the approved transcripts provided over 50,000 words of information on the topic. The shortest one was 2,200 while the longest was 6,600 words in length.

The Problems Arising From Two Different Types of Data

While the data from the interviews provided enough information to analyse the Australian perspective, a crucial fact that has to be kept in mind with respect to the comparison with the *Rechtsgutstheorie* is the different sources of information to be compared.

The *Rechtsgutstheorie* was presented by taking one elaborated concept as an example. Roxin's approach is set out in a textbook. It is a rather comprehensive narrative presentation. Due to the fact that information on the Australian perspective is not available in this form, it was mainly gained by semi-structured expert interviews in the form of oral statements that were made in reply to particular questions.

An attempt to minimize the differences in explanatory power resulting from the difference in the source of information is reflected in the methodology used for the interviews. First, the questions asked were open-ended in order to give the interviewees the opportunity to express their views comprehensively. Second, by sending the experts the questions in advance, the discrepancy between the two sources was further decreased as the interviewees had time to prepare their answers. Finally, all the experts were not only given the opportunity, but were also encouraged, to alter their statements when asked to approve the transcript of their interview.

Furthermore, it was determined that the data gained through the interviews would be utilized in the form of (sometimes long) direct quotes. In this manner, the context of the interviewees' statements is clear and the original wording is preserved. Therefore, instead of trying to generalize about the statements of different interviewees, the original statements are often provided as part of the analysis.

In spite of these measures taken to minimize the differences in the sources of knowledge, it is still necessary to keep this factor in mind, particularly because not all of the participants prepared themselves for the interviews and they did not all alter their statements. The information used to analyse the Australian perspective is therefore more specific because selective questions were asked, but also less generalizable as it was obtained through interviews with a group of experts.

Chapter 4
The Discussion in Australia

> But in Australia, no, it is just a lack of any sort of discussion on this at all. I cannot think of any good Australian paper, article or book on it at all.[1]

The aim of this chapter is to provide an analysis of how the question 'What sorts of conduct may the state legitimately make criminal?' is dealt with in Australia and to compare the approach identified with the German *Rechtsgutstheorie*.

In contrast to the German discussion, there is no single 'prevailing theory' on the limits of criminal law established in Australia. This is not because there were too many competing views advanced on the subject, but rather because of a lack of a normative discussion on the question in Australian academic writing.

Therefore, in contrast to the presentation of the German *Rechtsgutstheorie* in Chapter 2, the Australian perspective cannot be illustrated by using one elaborated concept as an example. Instead, the results of the interviews, as well as the existing literature on the topic, have to be analysed to provide information on two levels – the material and the formal. The former regards the *content* of the discussion, insofar as it is conducted (Several (Limiting) Principles), while the latter concerns the *way* in which the question on the limits of criminal law is dealt with in Australia (A Change towards Theory). Corresponding to the small scale of academic writing on the topic, the analysis does not aim to provide a detailed presentation of every single principle referred to in the discussion. Instead, it focuses on the formal level in order to emphasize that the crucial difference to the German approach is not the actual content, but rather the methodology applied. Thus, although both levels are analysed individually, their interdependence is also reflected in the following presentation of the principles applied, where links between the differing methods will be identified.

The analysis of the Australian discussion will lead to the conclusion that, while the differences to the *Rechtsgutstheorie* with regard to its substantive content are not crucial, the different methodologies applied in each country have fundamental consequences. It will be argued that, while the *Rechtsgutstheorie* provides German lawyers with a tool for legislative critique which is based on a legal argumentation, the emphasis in Australia on criminological considerations leads to a different understanding of the role of lawyers in the debate on the limits of criminal law (Jurisprudential Benefits: Legal Argumentation).

---

1 Interview with Dennis Baker (Sydney, 20 August 2007).

Several (Limiting) Principles

> I think the problem is my scepticism towards a grand theory and universalism that suggests that criminalization is polysemic, it has many different meanings attached to it, and it is multi-functional.[2]

> I doubt that there is any single criterion. I suspect, particularly in a pluralist society, there are many relevant considerations.[3]

In contrast to Germany, where one global theory is applied to determine the legitimate limits of the criminal law, the Australian scholars refer to several principles that are typically used for this purpose in Anglophone countries.[4] In the English-speaking discussion these different principles are not, in contrast to the *Rechtsgutstheorie*, considered to provide 'necessary conditions' for the criminalization of certain conduct, but only to give 'good reasons' for the state to do so.[5] This is a crucial difference between the two approaches. While the *Rechtsgutstheorie* leads to normative statements of 'right' or 'wrong' and 'legitimate' or 'illegitimate', depending on whether the necessary condition is met, the consideration of several principles that merely establish good reasons does not produce such absolute statements. If a particular offence does not meet the requirements of one principle, it can still be reasoned by another one. In this manner, the approach of invoking several principles instead of a single criterion leads to more differentiated results than the *Rechtsgutstheorie* because it acknowledges different motives for criminalization.[6] On the other hand, it does not lead to normative statements at all, as long as all of the invoked principles are considered to provide legitimate reasons for criminalization. Without a decision on which of the suggested principles themselves are legitimate tools to determine the limits of criminal law, the approach only provides a description of why a certain kind of behaviour is criminalized – it does not say whether this reason for criminalization is legitimate. In order to provide a tool for normative statements on the limits of criminal law using this approach, one has not only to analyse which

---

2 Interview with David Brown (Sydney, 13 August 2007).

3 Interview with Brent Fisse (Sydney, 22 August 2007).

4 See, for example, Joel Feinberg, *The Moral Limits of the Criminal Law* (Oxford University Press, New York 1984–1988); Andrew Ashworth, *Principles of Criminal Law* (5th edn Oxford University Press, Oxford 2006) 25–55.

5 The term 'good reasons' is used in particular by the American philosopher Joel Feinberg, *The Moral Limits*, n 4.

6 See Gerhard Seher, 'Prinzipiengestützte Strafnormlegitimation und der Rechtsgutbegriff' in Roland Hefendehl, Andrew von Hirsch and Wolfgang Wohlers (eds), *Die Rechstgutstheorie: Legitimationsbasis des Strafrechts oder dogmatisches Glasperlenspiel?* (Nomos, Baden-Baden 2003) 54.

offence can be explained by which principle, but also which of the principles can be accepted as a 'good reason'.

To use an easy and undisputed example: in order to make a normative statement on the legitimacy of the criminalization of homicide, this approach will first look for a principle that *explains* why it is illegal to kill someone. The harm principle will provide this explanation: homicide is criminalized in order to protect humans from being harmed (killed). The second step then is the evaluation of the principle's legitimacy; is the protection from harm a legitimate reason to criminalize conduct? The normative statement on the legitimacy of the criminalization of homicide then depends on how this second question is answered; only if the harm principle itself is considered to be legitimate can the criminalization of homicide be considered to be legitimate as well.

While this two-step method is a typical feature of the principle-based approach used in the whole English-speaking discussion, it must be kept in mind, particularly for the analysis of the Australian perspective. In the United States, as well as in the United Kingdom, the second step, the normative assessment of a principle's legitimacy, is dealt with in the academic literature.[7] And while these authors are also acknowledged in the Australian discussion, Australian authors themselves do not generally take the second step in their academic writing. Thus, the principles invoked are not used to proclaim limits for the criminal law, but only to *describ*e its actual content.[8]

Accordingly, many of the criminal lawyers interviewed – mostly practitioners, but also academics – 'do not have a clear understanding of the phrase "the limits of criminal law"',[9] at least not in the theoretical, normative sense.

> I do not really understand the concept at all, so far as it depends upon judicial determination. … So when you ask what is the limits of criminal law, it is what the law says, is the criminal law.[10]

> The rule of thumb is that there are not any limits. You can do whatever you like. If you want to pass an act, which says that black is white, you can do it. We do not have a bill of rights in this country. So, we have very little in [the] way of judicial supervision of legislative programs. There have been very few occasions on which the High Court as a constitutional authority struck down

---

7 For the United States see particularly Feinberg, *The Moral Limits*, above n 4; Douglas Husak, *Overcriminalization: The Limits of the Criminal Law* (Oxford University Press, New York 2008). For the United Kingdom see, for example, Ashworth, above n 4, 22–55; A.P. Simester and Andrew von Hirsch, 'Rethinking the Offense Principle' (2002) 8 *Legal Theory* 269.

8 This characteristic of the Australian approach is dealt with in detail below p. 73 et seq.

9 Interview with Stephen Odgers (Sydney, 27 August 2007).

10 Interview with Sir Gerard Brennan (Sydney, 15 August 2007).

> state legislation – [they] could be counted on the fingers of one hand – in terms of the limits of criminal law. There are, of course, lots and lots of inconsistencies with Commonwealth law and all that sort of [thing] – but not in terms of the limits of the criminal law. So, by and large, if you are cunning enough you can do whatever you please – and states do.[11]

> Actually, I do not see that many limits. The most important limit I can think of is that there must be a justiciable issue. ... The only other limits I see are essentially political and conventional in the sense that the legislature is inhibited by established conventions from making certain kinds of criminal law. As, for example, the conventions against retrospective legislation, the requirement of jury trial for serious offences and the requirement of proof beyond reasonable doubt. But the conventions are always changing and very few have constitutional protection in this country. Each of the conventions I have mentioned can be disregarded by Australian legislatures.[12]

On the other hand, some of the Australian criminal lawyers actually consider the question about the limits of criminal law in the same way as it is understood in the German discussion – 'a policy question, as to what should be the limits. In other words, to what extent should the criminal law be used as a means of social control?'[13]

> It is not actually a term of art in the criminal law, but in the academic understanding it is usually used in a questioning sense to say, to what extent should the criminal law be used as the means of enforcement of social norms?[14]

> I see the limits of the criminal law as being some exercise which tries to confine criminal law within some proper or appropriate sphere of activity.[15]

A very clear understanding of the term was presented by one of the interviewed academics:

> I suppose we are talking about the restrictions that apply to criminalization: when we feel that there is no justification for structuring a prohibition as a crime, as distinct from any other legal wrong. It would usually be framed in theoretical terms, in a range of principles that scholars have worked on over time, like the harm principle, which considers harm to others. Enforcement of morals structures crimes around 'serious wrongs', and 'wrongfulness' being something

11 Interview with Matthew Goode (Adelaide, 14 August 2007).
12 Interview with Ian Leader-Elliott (Adelaide, 14 August 2007).
13 Interview with Brent Fisse (Sydney, 22 August 2007).
14 Interview with David Weisbrot (Sydney, 12 September 2007).
15 Interview with David Brown (Sydney, 13 August 2007).

> that has a moral and a sociocultural dimension, recognizing that in different places and different times and different cultures different things would be regarded as 'wrong'. There are a number of different liberal and moral theories of criminalization that seek to cut down the scope of criminal law.[16]

And finally, one of the interviewed academics stated that he actually focuses on this question in his research.[17] Asked about his general understanding of the phrase, Dennis Baker provided the following description, which includes normative as well as constitutional thoughts:

> What I look at is the moral limits. That is, looking at the moral content of the criminal law. Generally speaking, Andrew Ashworth, a professor at Oxford, wrote a little article a few years ago: 'Is the Criminal Law a Lost Cause?' It does not do a lot, but what it does do is identify that there really is no moral content in the criminal law. If you look at the history of any common law jurisdiction, if you do a comparison to the civil law (private wrongs) jurisdiction you see that in the common law criminal law has evolved out of one body of wrongs. So a lot of these things are civil wrongs and then it became a problem with the King's peace and the Crown was at a state where it was, you know, the King lost a man. It was regarded not only as that person's loss but also a loss for the King and the Crown. Then the Crown started taking on the role of enforcing some of these remedies against the wrongs. So then it became the prosecution's role and, generally, in more recent time, commentators summed that up in a basic statement like: 'The criminal law tries to deal with wrongs that are not safe to leave to the redress of the private parties involved. That is where it is in the public or collective interest for the state to take a role as well.'
>
> Following on from that we see why the current state of the criminal law does not really have a moral content. Back to my comments about penal populism, groups such as beggars, which I have written on, are criminalized for no good reason. They do not harm others – they cause offence to those who do not understand their disabilities. What is the moral reason for continuing to criminalize begging after 800 years? If we look at the history of it we can see why it has been a crime. But you see plenty of these crimes; public nudity does not fit in with the harm principle, and again, it raises a question about the moral content of criminalization: what is the objective rather than positive moral justification for criminalizing it.

---

16 Interview with a professor of law at an Australian university (30 August 2007).

17 See, for example, Dennis J. Baker, 'The Moral Limits of Criminalizing Remote Harms' (2007) 10(3) *New Criminal Law Review* 370; Dennis J. Baker, 'The Harm Principle vs Kantian Criteria for Ensuring Fair, Principled and Just Criminalisation' (2008) 33 *Australian Journal of Legal Philosophy* 1; Dennis J. Baker, 'The Sense and Nonsense of Criminalising Transfers of Obscene Material' (2008) 26 *Singapore Law Review* 126.

> Positive morality is morality according to what the community thinks is right. So community at a given place and time might say that it is fine to criminalize homosexuals. That is the old conventional harm (relativistic/community/legal moralism) argument produced by Patrick Devlin. Hart counteracted that argument by saying that we need some objective standards to ensure that criminalization decisions meet some sort of standard of fairness. But we see that has not been applied in practice. As I said, with homosexuals it was only in 2003 in the Supreme Court case in the United States (*Lawrence v Texas*[18]) that they decided to use a privacy right to protect homosexuality.
>
> Also, while I am on that point, it brings the whole idea of human rights, which in our jurisdictions has, in practice, the most impact. Basically, things like free speech have been used in America and Canada to decriminalize begging, which has been found to involve the free speech right. Privacy right has been used to decriminalize homosexuality in the US, but then it has not protected people going to strip clubs. Possessing sex toys is also an offence in some states in the US and the privacy right, which is a constitutional right, is that the discretion of the court? Even though it is sort of a critical moral norm, privacy. But it is at the discretion of the court and they can decide from time to time what they decide it is. And it varies, depending on who is on the court at a time.[19]

Also noteworthy is the answer given by Sir Michael Kirby, who was the only practising lawyer to articulate his own, normative point of view on the question:

> It is exactly 50 years ago since the report of the Wolfenden Committee – an inquiry on homosexual offences and prostitution – was published in the United Kingdom. That committee had to address exactly this question: 'What are the limits of the criminal law?' The report of the Committee recommended the abolition of the criminal offences, directed at homosexual men who are adults, occurring in private. This became extremely influential throughout the Commonwealth of Nations. It led, 10 years later, to the enactment of reforms of the law of the United Kingdom. That led, in due course, in the manner of those times, to changes throughout the Commonwealth of Nations, including ultimately in Australia where, eventually by a long and tortuous process, all of the old criminal laws were abolished.
>
> I received word this morning that the Court of Final Appeal in Hong Kong this month held that the anti-sodomy laws of Hong Kong in their application to a semi-public place are unconstitutional in Hong Kong. So the process of reform continues. It is a process of defining the limits of criminal law.
>
> As a result of the Wolfenden Committee report there was a major debate about this subject in Britain. The debate was led on the side of the abolitionists by Professor H.L.A. Hart. It was led on the side of the retentionists by Lord Devlin.

---

18 539 U.S. 558(2003).

19 Interview with Dennis Baker (Sydney, 20 August 2007).

> Lord Devlin asserted that it was every society's right to express criminal law as dealing with matters which society found repulsive and unacceptable for its own wellbeing. H.L.A. Hart (who it later emerged was bisexual) was in favour of abolition on the ground that there are some things which, as the Wolfenden report stated: 'putting it quite bluntly, are not the proper business of the law.' I align myself with Wolfenden and with H.L.A. Hart. I believe that most informed people nowadays do. I was reading a book on the aftermath of the Wolfenden report when I was in England last week. It showed that, ultimately, Lord Devlin voted for the abolition of the offences. So he apparently, ultimately, came round, 10 years later, to the belief that the law should be changed.
>
> All of this is generality. And it does not really describe with precision where the limits lie. But essentially, the view that was advanced long ago in the English legal tradition, by Bentham and Mill, appears to have gained ascendency: activities which are 'self-regarding' are not legitimately the law's business. Activities which are 'other-regarding' and affect other people are the law's legitimate business. Matters do not become 'other-regarding' simply because some people feel very upset by the activities of others in society. If we were to adopt that principle, we would allow our law to punish and stigmatize vulnerable minorities simply because some people get upset with their behaviour, although not personally affected by it.[20]

When, in the following sections of this book, an overview of the principles referred to in the contemporary Australian discussion is given, it is crucial to take these different understandings of the phrase 'the limits of criminal law' into consideration. Ultimately, the analysis will show that the Australian discussion is highly contextualized, and that most of the interviewees are referring to contextual variables rather than making absolute statements (as they are typically made with respect to the *Rechtsgutstheorie*).

The Harm Principle

The protection from harm appears to be the most prevalent principle to describe (and limit) the scope of the criminal law in Australia.[21] In its original version, as articulated by John Stuart Mill, it states that 'the only purpose for which power

20 Interview with Sir Michael Kirby (Sydney, 24 July 2007).

21 See, for example, Simon Bronitt and Bernadette McSherry, *Principles of Criminal Law* (2nd edn Thomson Lawbook, Pyrmont 2005) 52–54; David Brown et al., *Brown, Farrier, Neal and Weisbrot's Criminal Laws: Materials and Commentary on Criminal Law and Process of New South Wales* (4th edn Federation Press, Leichhardt 2006) 88–91; Bernadette McSherry and Bronwyn Naylor, *Australian Criminal Law: Critical Perspectives* (Oxford University Press, Melbourne 2004) 18–19; Mark Findlay, Stephen Odgers and Stanley Yeo, *Australian Criminal Justice* (3rd edn Oxford University Press, South Melbourne 2005) 3–4.

can be rightfully exercised over any member of a civilised community, against his will, is to prevent harm to others.'[22] While Mill did not restrict his argument to the criminal law, but applied it to any state action, today the harm principle in particular is used to limit the scope of the criminal law.

The main problem generally associated with this approach is the definition of the term 'harm to others'.[23]

> The problem with it always has been the indeterminacy of 'harm to others', particularly when you move from core harm to indirect harms. The concept of harm is problematic; is it anthropocentric, is it human-focused or is it environmental? Does it extend to indirect harm? And so on. You can think about any debate in relation to pornography and you will see that issue. …
>
> It is as valid as any other principle. It just comes down to how broad or narrowly you are going to construct harm. As soon as you start broadening it out it loses much of its liberty enhancing features. In a truly classical way you want to confine harm in a fairly narrow, physical conception. But, of course, in a modern psychological area, ideas of emotional harm, distress, discrimination and all these other kinds of 'harms' are developed and obviously that much more, effectively, broadens the scope of criminal law.[24]

Because of the lack of a recognized definition of the term, the principle is often considered as not being able to limit the scope of the criminal law, and furthermore perhaps even to further its expansion.[25]

> In almost any circumstance you could probably reason your way out of the harm principle, if you were really looking to do that. If you are a libertarian you can probably construe it more narrowly and look just at that particular individual. If you are someone who believes in a broader reach of the state then it is very easy to broaden it. We are even starting to use the arguments now about obesity. People say [that] obese people are a drain upon the state. They should be given less opportunity to have access to the health system and those kinds of things. It depends upon your basic philosophical approach whether you want to contain the principle or whether you want to go further. Even where you can say that the conduct clearly affects others there are still questions about whether the criminal sanction is the most effective one. It really depends on what you want to do.[26]

---

22 John Stuart Mill, *On Liberty* (Penguin, London 1985, first published 1859) 68.

23 See, for example, Bronitt and McSherry, above n 21, 53–54; McSherry and Naylor, above n 21, 19.

24 Interview with a professor of law at an Australian university (30 August 2007).

25 See Findlay, Odgers and Yeo, above n 21, 4.

26 Interview with David Weisbrot (Sydney, 12 September 2007).

> I think with the harm principle, almost anything can be characterized as a 'harm'. The range of things that can be counted as harms are being daily expanded as new forms of harm are invented or discovered. In that sense I do not see the harm principle as a limit, but rather as a principle of expansion of the criminal law.[27]

Interviewee Dennis Baker presented his own approach to the harm principle. He considers it to be the most important limiting principle, although it has to be regarded as part of a greater principle, the 'fairness principle'. One of the problems he sees is the required intensity of harm:

> What is not controversial is the harm principle. Because most people would agree that it is an objective standard. If you harm someone and if you wrongfully harm them, that is if you have culpability and intend to wrongfully harm them rather than just harm them by accident, then we could say it is fair, in most cases, to invoke the criminal law. The great problem there is measuring harm. We have trivial wrongs like littering and then we have collective harm. But then you also have minor harms to a billionaire who loses five cents. Can you really say he is 'harmed'?
>
> Basically we are arguing now there, according to Feinberg, that you protect the billionaire's interests, even though he might not be harmed significantly by losing five cents, because it upholds the whole idea of property rights. And the system of property rights alone is something that we need to protect. Without [which] we are harmed …
>
> I argue, and it is coming out in the forthcoming paper, that the harm principle does not provide the sole objective criterion for ensuring fair criminalization; it is not capable of justifying the criminalization of all those objective wrongs that are properly criminalizable. Many criminal theorists go wrong by assuming it can do all the work. It is a part of a greater principle called the 'fairness principle', which is my own principle [that] I am inventing. The fairness principle would hold that you do not criminalize unless you have reasons that demonstrated it is fair and those reasons need to be objective, as I just said. They need at least to accord with some sense of objectiveness. I argue, within that is a subset of principles and the harm principle is one of them. By and large the harm principle will do most of the work to show why it is fair to invoke the criminal law.[28]

A further criticism of the principle, which is often articulated, is its incapacity to explain why the 'deterrent effect of the criminal law should be applied to ensure that safety belts are worn by drivers, or that motorcyclists should wear helmets.'[29]

---

27 Interview with Ian Leader-Elliott (Adelaide, 14 August 2007).

28 Interview with Dennis Baker (Sydney, 20 August 2007).

29 Findlay, Odgers and Yeo, above n 21, 4.

An additional problem which the harm principle, in its original version, faces is that it does not protect animals.

> Cruelty to animals is not protected by harm. I do not think that is a huge problem. I think that it just needs to be addressed in a further paper. Animals cannot have rights, obviously, but we can have duties to animals and Joseph Raz (a professor from Oxford) argued that, I think convincingly. The concept of harm is still there; it is just that we say in that case we have a duty not to harm animals rather than the animal has a right not to be harmed.[30]

The problems described above surrounding the correct definition of 'harm to others', the difficulty concerning an explanation for regulations on safety belts and helmets, as well as the consideration of animals, are similar to the issues dealt with in the German discussion. The question of the required intensity of harm to a *Rechtsgut* is also raised in Germany. These questions are dealt with under the heading 'subsidiarity', and with respect to the prescribed wearing of seat belts and helmets, German law's distinction between criminal and administrative offences comes into play.[31] The potential indirect harm discussed in relation to these issues[32] is only considered to legitimate the use of administrative offences – not the criminal law.

Similar to the problems surrounding the definition of 'harm', the definition of the term *Rechtsgut* is, as we have seen, heavily disputed and the protection of animals, too, can only be achieved by altering the concept.

The consequences arising from these issues are, however, different. In Germany, the concept in general is considered to provide legitimate answers, despite different opinions on the right definition of the crucial term. The argument about the correct definition of *Rechtsgut* is part of the academic discussion and the differences are considered to be fewer than the similarities. In Australia, disagreement on the scope of the term 'harm to others' leads to a broad opposition to the whole concept. Instead of a discussion of the correct definition of harm, one finds only statements about the problems caused by the lack of an established definition.

Interestingly, the *presentation* of the harm principle sometimes also appears similar to the way in which the *Rechtsgutstheorie* is constructed. Findlay et al. state that '[t]he overall aim of the criminal law is the prevention of certain kinds of behaviour that society regards as either harmful or potentially harmful.'[33] This approach seems to be very similar to the methodology used by the German *Rechtsgutstheorie* since it proclaims a major aim of the criminal law – the prevention of (potentially) harmful behaviour. The crucial difference is that the

30 Interview with Dennis Baker (Sydney, 20 August 2007).

31 See above p. 18.

32 See, for example, Findlay, Odgers and Yeo, above n 21, 4.

33 Ibid., 2.

authors do not draw the conclusion that this overall aim could also provide a clear argument to determine the limits of criminal law.

> The criminal law is applied by society as a defence against harms that injure the interests and values that are considered fundamental to its proper functioning. These interests and values cover a wide area. They include the bodily integrity of people, the security of property, protection of the environment and moral values.[34]

By including moral values in the scope of interests and values that are protected by the criminal law, the term harm is not used in its limiting function, but only to describe what is considered to be the reality of the criminal law as it stands. Harm, in this sense, only describes any negative effect on any protected interest or value; it does not say which of them *ought* to be protected from harm.

Another presentation of the harm principle that is similar to the structure of the *Rechtsgutstheorie* is given by Brown et al.:

> A number of writers think that the characteristic shared by all forms of criminal action is that they are harmful. An important corollary of this view is that *only* harmful acts should be criminal. Harm has immediate plausibility as a justification for criminalising a given form of behaviour. The term has a commonsense ring to it and connotations of objectivity, simplicity and concreteness which belie its complexity. Harm is a concept which needs to be examined carefully. What does it mean to cause *harm*? Should all forms of harmful behaviour be criminalised?[35]

Again, there are obvious similarities to the way in which the *Rechtsgutstheorie* is articulated. However, differences to the German theory also become evident. First, the introductory phrase in the quotation raises the question: what is meant by 'criminal action'? It cannot be the formal, legal definition of crime, which is used by the *Rechtsgutstheorie*, because if all the forms of behaviour that are criminalized by the state already share the characteristic that they are harmful, it does not make any sense to claim that '*only* harmful acts should be criminal', since that would already be the case. Therefore, the definition of 'crime' in the first sentence of the quote has to be a criminological, material one. As such, the criminological answer to the question of what constitutes crime calls for the actual criminal law to be limited to harmful behaviour. Because this postulation is based on a criminological concept, it functions differently to the *Rechtsgutstheorie*. The last sentence of the quotation, 'Should all forms of harmful behaviour be criminalised?', is proof of that. The German theory acknowledges that it can only describe the *limits* of criminal law – not its total content. In other words, the *Rechtsgutstheorie* can only answer the question 'What should *not* be criminalized?' It cannot and does not seek

34 Ibid.

35 Brown et al., above n 21, 88.

to say what *should* be criminalized. This is due to the fact that it is a restrictive concept – it aims to restrict the power of the state to interfere with the liberty of the citizens. But it is not a concept which can be used to identify what a crime actually is. Which kinds of behaviour that endanger or harm a *Rechtsgut* and that the state decides to criminalize is – indeed – considered to be a political question. The *Rechtsgutstheorie* only tells the legislature what should *not* be criminalized. While this is seen as a fundamental characteristic of the theory in Germany,[36] it is regarded to be a flaw of such concepts in Australia.[37]

> One of the problems with all these theories, whether it is the harm principle or what I just described, is that they tell us when not to criminalize but they do not really tell us when we should criminalize.[38]

One can only consider this as being a 'problem with all these theories' if one expects them to give answers to questions which they were not developed to address. Only if one expects the concept to give a criminological answer to the question 'What is a crime?' can one legitimately argue that it is flawed because it can only say what should not be criminalized. If one asks, instead, the jurisprudential question about the legitimate limits of the criminal law, the harm principle provides significant answers to this question. The criminological framework in which the discussion of the harm principle is embedded leads to a misunderstanding of the function of a limiting concept.[39]

In Bronitt and McSherry's *Principles of Criminal Law*,[40] the authors make a promising distinction between the criminal law as it stands and the 'reconstruction of the criminal law'. This division is promising because it allows consideration of the two-step method of principle-based discussion on the limits of the criminal law: first, analysis of the reasons for criminalization, and second, making a determination on whether these reasons are legitimate. However, by arguing 'the search for a single unifying theory that can explain or guide our decisions to proscribe behaviour as criminal is pointless'[41] in the context of presenting the harm principle, the authors suggest that the principle was intended to identify behaviour that can be called 'criminal' but cannot fulfil this function.

In fact, the harm principle is not supposed to provide answers to the criminological question 'What is a crime?' Like the *Rechtsgutstheorie*, it only

36 Claus Roxin, *Strafrecht, Allgemeiner Teil, Band I: Grundlagen, Aufbau der Verbrechenslehre* (4th edn C.H. Beck, Munich 2006) 13–14.

37 McSherry and Naylor, above n 21, 19.

38 Interview with a professor of law at an Australian university (30 August 2007).

39 This correlation is analysed in detail below p. 81 et seq.

40 Bronitt and McSherry, above n 21, 51.

41 Ibid., referring to Paul McCutcheon, 'Morality and the Criminal Law: Reflections on Hart-Devlin' (2002) 47 *Criminal Law Quarterly* 15, 37–38. Also see McSherry and Naylor, above n 21, 22.

provides answers to the jurisprudential question 'What kinds of behaviour should not be criminalized?' or, formulated in the positive, 'What sorts of conduct can the state *legitimately* make criminal?' Only this understanding of the function of the harm principle accords with its function as originally outlined by Mill. Mill aimed to assert a 'principle, by which the propriety or impropriety of government interference is customarily tested.'[42] The principle was not developed to test if the government *should* interfere – but to test whether a given interference is legitimate.

The reason Australian criminal lawyers do not make a clear distinction between the two questions – one is never considered in detachment from the other – is based on the general mixing of criminology on the one hand and jurisprudential criminal law theory on the other.[43] This is why the harm principle's incapacity to answer a criminological question is considered a flaw in the concept and this is why the harm principle does not enjoy the status the *Rechtsgutstheorie* has in Germany. The difficulty in defining the term harm to others, on the other hand, does not reveal why the harm principle is not the acknowledged and applicable concept for determining the limits of criminal law. The term *Rechtsgut* faces the same problems, but the controversy surrounding its correct definition is part of the discussion; it does not hinder the debate or the acceptance of the concept as a legitimate tool for establishing the limits of criminal law.

The Offence Principle

The American philosopher Joel Feinberg distinguished between 'harm to others' and 'offence to others'.[44] In contrast to Mill, who only accepted a single purpose for state coercion – the prevention of harm to others – Feinberg acknowledges two good reasons.

The crucial point made by Feinberg is that certain behaviour, though it does not fall within his definition of harmful conduct, can nevertheless be legitimately criminalized because of its offensive nature. However, in contrast to harmful conduct, offensive behaviour does not always provide a reason for legitimate criminalization. The intensity, duration and inescapability, as well as motivation and social acceptance of the offensive behaviour, must be considered.[45]

It could be argued that Feinberg's offence principle aims to correct the effect of his definition of harm, which proves too narrow to encompass every form of behaviour he wanted to fall within the category of legitimate criminalization.[46]

---

42 Mill, above n 22, 67.

43 This is dealt with in detail below p. 81 et seq.

44 Joel Feinberg, *Offense to Others* (Oxford University Press, New York 1985).

45 See ibid., 35 and 44.

46 For a different approach to Feinberg's concept that suggests that all cases in which offence can legitimately be criminalized also involve harm, see Simester and von Hirsch, above n 7.

Nonetheless, in the Australian discussion, Feinberg's offence principle does not play a role at all. It is not dealt with in the Australian texts and only one of the interviewees mentioned it as being part of his research interests:

> Outside of that I have looked at Feinberg's offense principle but I have not, at this stage, concluded that it might be a reason for saying it is fair to invoke the criminal law. I am working on that at the moment, but I am reading a whole lot of stuff on ethics because, as I said, there is a conflict there because it seems to be 'offense' is determined solely by positive morality or what I call 'conventional morality'. That is, whatever we decide in this community is offensive is what we determine it by and it might not universally be wrongful.[47]

Asked about whether they knew about Feinberg's theory eight of the 11 interviewees stated that they were not familiar with his work on the limits of criminal law.

On the other hand, 'offensiveness as a ground for criminal prohibition' is regarded as forming 'the basis of a range of existing criminal prohibitions in what are referred to as public order offences.'[48] Interestingly, the discussion of this does not refer to the harm principle, as Feinberg has, but is connected to immorality as a reason for criminalization.

> Debates on offensiveness as a ground for criminal prohibition often proceed in close association with debates about immorality. For example, they are frequently concerned with sexual behaviour. However, some important differences are worth noticing. First, offensive behaviour in law involves an element of publicness, although, as we will see, the definition of public place is very broad. Acts that positive morality allows in private might be regarded as offensive if done in public (e.g., heterosexual intercourse between married couples). Second, it is possible for society to view behaviour as legally permissible, though immoral, when carried out in private, but legally impermissible, because offensive, if carried out in public (e.g., homosexual intercourse between consenting adults). In both these cases publicness rather than immorality is the heart of the concern. In this they are more readily assimilable to the case of harm since the interests of third parties may be adversely affected (i.e., some identifiable or hypothetical individual may be offended by the sight of the behaviour). Immoral behaviour carried out in private between consenting adults does not so readily share this characteristic unless there is a very broad definition of what counts as a harm.[49]

The main problem of offensiveness as a legitimate reason for criminalization is seen in the historic changes of what is considered to be offensive or immoral.[50]

---

47 Interview with Dennis Baker (Sydney, 20 August 2007).

48 Brown et al., above n 21, 95, without reference to Feinberg.

49 Ibid.

50 Ibid., 97–98.

> However, the basic schema is, I think, clear. If activity is truly to be categorized as self-regarding it is, as Wolfenden said, putting it bluntly, not the law's business. And it does not become the law's business simply because there are people in society who feel very upset about such activity. The range of things about which people get upset changes over time. Blasphemy is a good example. In medieval England it was a most grave offence. In some parts of the Islamic world today it is a very serious offence. But in most modern Western societies it would not be regarded as an offence at all, and certainly not one calling for strong punishments. So these things change. It is a mistake to think they are set in stone. This illustrates the fact that you can have broad principles; but applying them will lead to different outcomes in different people and over different intervals of time.[51]

In the German discussion, offensiveness is again debated within the framework of the *Rechtsgutstheorie*. Similar to Feinberg's approach, offensive behaviour is only considered to provide a reason for criminalization under special circumstances. As mentioned above, the German theory does not focus on definitions of offensiveness, but on goods/interests that ought to be protected from being harmed by offensive conduct. What these goods/interests have in common is that they are personal feelings, which, it is argued, only ought to be protected from conduct that can cause feelings of being threatened. Thus, in terms of the *Rechtsgutstheorie*, offensiveness per se is not generally considered to legitimate a criminal offence unless the conduct is likely to cause fear of, for example, a sexual assault.

Morality

> I think, therefore, that it is not possible to set theoretical limits to the power of the State to legislate against immorality. It is not possible to settle in advance exceptions to the general rule or to define inflexibly areas of morality into which the law is in no circumstances to be allowed to enter.[52]

The Australian discussion on morality as a reason for criminalization is still mainly influenced by the Hart-Devlin debate.[53] But while it is widely acknowledged today that 'public morality … is not a sufficient reason in itself; for all the old reasons

---

51 Interview with Sir Michael Kirby (Sydney, 24 July 2007).

52 Lord Patrick Devlin, *The Enforcement of Morals* (Oxford University Press, London 1965) 12–13.

53 See, for example, Brown et al., above n 21, 91–94; Bronitt and McSherry, above n 21, 55–58; McSherry and Naylor, above n 21, 20–21; Findlay, Odgers and Yeo, above n 21, 3.

that were stated in that Hart-Devlin debate and in such kinds of debates',[54] morality is considered to have major influence on the criminal legislation in practice.

> There has been a real turnaround from the liberalism of the 1960s and a huge increase in legislation about sexual morality. I refer in particular to the extended applications of legislation creating offences relating to internet child pornography. These offences will catch, of course, cases that do involve harm to individuals, in the sense that there are real children involved. But in Australia and in many other countries no distinction is drawn between child pornography, which has a real child victim, and child pornography, which has a simulated, computer-generated image of a child. Though the ostensible reason for the law is the protection of child victims I think the real focus of concern is not the remote victim in Russia or China or some other country where the images were made. The real focus of concern is about the moral depravity of the individual who is watching this stuff.[55]

On the other hand, some of the Australian writers agree with Paul McCutcheon,[56] saying that even the concept of harm is morally loaded 'with the effect that the designation of a consequence as a "harm" involves a societal judgement with moral dimensions.'[57] However, even when quoting his work,[58] none of the Australian texts follows McCutcheon in his finding that '[i]n short, the law-maker may properly justify a prohibition on an appeal to moral reason.'[59] Having said that, the statement is not critiqued – it is simply quoted.

In summary, independent of the distinction made between 'positive' and 'critical morality', the moral wrongness of behaviour in itself is not generally considered to provide a legitimate reason for criminalization.

> If, on the other hand, the conduct, which may not be in accordance with the moral standards of the majority of the community, but it does not have any effect other than disturbing the preconceptions of that majority, then I would say there is no justification for criminalization. But what that comes down to, I guess, is that you cannot legislate for conduct or proscribe conduct in such a way as to preclude the virtue of individuals and transform it merely into legal conformism. We might all think that giving away your goods to feed the poor

54 Interview with Brent Fisse (Sydney, 2 August 2007); also interview with Nicolas Cowdery (Sydney, 13 August 2007); interview with Ian Leader-Elliott (Adelaide, 14 August 2007).

55 Interview with Ian Leader-Elliott (Adelaide, 14 August 2007).

56 McCutcheon, above n 41, 22.

57 Bronitt and McSherry, above n 21, 54; also see McSherry and Naylor, above n 21, 21.

58 Bronitt and McSherry, above n 21, 57.

59 McCutcheon, above n 41, 16.

> is a highly moral thing to do, but one would never think of proscribing conduct which consists of not giving away your goods to feed the poor. And if you were to take the law to that extent then, of course, you would find that there is no room left for morality, only for law. That would be a mortal blow to any concept of human dignity.[60]

However, morality is used to describe legislative motives for individual prohibitions – especially in the area of sexual conduct.[61] Thus, with regard to morality, the German and the Australian approaches are similar in that one of the most important consequences of the *Rechtsgutstheorie* is that the immorality of an act does not legitimate its criminalization. What is different, again, is the framework within which the argument is held. The *Rechtsgutstheorie* strictly rejects moral arguments by claiming that immoral conduct does not endanger safe and peaceful coexistence. In Australia, on the other hand, morality is presented as a principle that historically had and still has a major influence on the criminal law and is therefore able to explain many offences in the law in force. And although most of the interviewed criminal lawyers considered immorality of behaviour not to be a sufficient reason for criminalization, the textbook presentation of the topic does not provide such clear statements. Once again, the Australian texts focus on the practical influence that morality had and has on the criminal law rather than presenting normative statements on its legitimacy as a reason for criminalization.[62]

The Welfare Principle

> Certainly, welfare, likewise, is something that is (depending how it is defined), obviously, striving to promote the welfare of the majority (to put it in Benthamite terms). It certainly is a well established principle.[63]

In contrast to the harm principle, which is based on individual autonomy, the welfare principle states that '[w]hat is, or should be considered, a crime depends upon an evaluation of what is "best" for society as a whole.'[64]

Advocates of the welfare principle – in order to determine what is best for society as a whole and therefore what should be protected by the criminal law – refer to the 'values, needs and interests which a society has decided through its democratic processes are fundamental to its collective social functioning'.[65] The

---

60 Interview with Sir Gerard Brennan (Sydney, 15 August 2007).

61 See, for example, Bronitt and McSherry, above n 21, 57.

62 See, for example, Brown et al., above n 21, 91–94; McSherry and Naylor, above n 21, 19–21; Bronitt and McSherry, above n 21, 54–58.

63 Interview with a professor of law at an Australian university (30 August 2007).

64 Bronitt and McSherry, above n 21, 60–61.

65 See ibid., 61.

Australian texts[66] that mention public welfare as a limiting principle refer to the works by Anders Vilhelm Lundstedt[67] and Nicola Lacey.[68]

Behaviour, like drug use or environmental pollution, can legitimately be criminalized according to this principle.[69] Although this approach seems to contrast strongly with the autonomy-based harm principle, it has also been suggested that both principles 'may work towards the same end'.[70] This understanding considers autonomy to require a 'positive social freedom' rather than just a 'negative individual freedom'.[71]

The only communality between the welfare principle and the *Rechtsgutstheorie* lies in the acceptance that certain values of society and the state are legitimate goods/interests that ought to be protected by the criminal law. As shown above, the *Rechtsgutstheori*e, even in its most individualized version, also acknowledges *Kollektivrechtsgüter* (for example, the functioning of the judicature, the monetary system or the general safety of road traffic). These goods/interests are also necessary for public welfare and can therefore also be protected according to this principle.

The major difference between the two concepts is the fact that the (classic) welfare principle *only* considers what is best for society as a whole, while the *Rechtsgutstheorie* includes *Kollektivrechtsgüter* because they are essential for the free and peaceful development of individual personality. The starting points for each theory – society on the one hand and the individual on the other – are therefore different.

The welfare principle therefore has more in common with Amelung's concept, which refers to protection from anti-social behaviour.[72] As we have seen, Amelung tries to limit the consequences of his concept for the individual by acknowledging fundamental constitutional values like human dignity and personal freedom. This attempt, which ultimately leads to results similar to those produced by the *Rechtsgutstheorie,* is comparable to the previously suggested integration of the (individual focused) harm principle and the (society focused) welfare principle.

66 See ibid., 60–62; McSherry and Naylor, above n 21, 21–22; Findlay, Odgers and Yeo, above n 21, 45.

67 Anders Vilhelm Lundstedt, *Legal Thinking Revised: My Views on Law* (Almqvist and Wiksell, Stockholm 1956). The Australian texts for some reason always call the book *Legal Thinking Revisited.*

68 Nicola Lacey, *State Punishment: Political Principles and Community Values* (Routledge, London, New York 1988).

69 See Bronitt and McSherry, above n 21, 61.

70 Ashworth, above n 4, 29.

71 Ibid., 28–29. See also Bronitt and McSherry, above n 21, 62.

72 See above p. 25–26.

The Public Interest

> Rather than appeal to divinely inspired abstract moral principles, modern judges and lawyers justify the criminal law in secular terms of the interest and values of 'the public'. While appearing to be neutral and objective, the public interest is a highly political concept.[73]

In their criminal law textbook, Brown et al. draw a distinction between public and private interests in relation to the differentiation between crimes and torts.

> The problem here is that most interests can be expressed either as public or private. ... In short, while the public/private distinction has some appeal, it does not go far enough in helping us to understand the phenomenon of crime. Nor does it go far enough to explain the complex public responses to breaches of certain interests.[74]

The only other text to mention public interest as a principle to justify criminalization[75] is that of Bronitt and McSherry. Here, public interest is put on the same level as public opinion; it is considered to be 'malleable', but also to have significant (political) influence.

> The difficulty with using concepts like public interest or public opinion is that they are neither neutral nor autonomous. They are highly contingent upon historical, political and social contexts. Responses to particular conduct are often shaped by moral panics and the politics of law and order. ... While public interest or public opinion are malleable concepts, and thus dubious guides for criminalisation, they have considerable symbolic and rhetorical force.[76]

While in Australia the public interest is never presented as a legitimate reason for criminalization, it is considered to play an influential role in legislative decisions.

In Germany, the topic that deals with the political influence of public opinion is 'symbolic legislation'.[77] While, like in Australia, the attractiveness of such considerations to politicians is acknowledged, the *Rechtsgutstheorie* clearly rejects them as legitimate reasons for criminalization.

Thus, while public opinion is presented as having significant influence on the legislation in both countries, the Australian texts do not make normative statements

---

73 Bronitt and McSherry, above n 21, 58.

74 Brown et al., above n 21, 86.

75 For the important relationship between public interest and sentencing see Findlay, Odgers and Yeo, above n 21, 283–286.

76 Bronitt and McSherry, above n 21, 60.

77 See above p. 14–15.

on the legitimacy of such considerations. Once again, they only describe the effects and problems of such motivations for criminalization.

Paternalism

Feinberg concluded that 'harm to self' does not provide a good reason for criminalization. The principle that does justify such prohibitions is paternalism[78] – the state protects the individual from him or herself. The debates on paternalism concern the limits of consent to obviate punishability. Classic areas include the consumption of illicit drugs and other consensual harmful behaviour like prizefighting or sadomasochistic sexual practices. Interestingly, paternalism as a justificatory principle is neither promoted nor rejected in the Australian literature – it is simply not discussed at all.[79] Instead, the principle of morality is invoked in such cases.[80]

Asked about the role of consent in sexual conduct, some of the interviewees, explicitly or by implication, rejected the idea of paternalism as a legitimate reason for criminalization. But although the majority of the experts did not mention the term paternalism, most of them indirectly rejected the principle by arguing that genuine and proper consent should rule out criminalization.

> And it is hard, ultimately, to get away in a pluralistic society from having some pursuit of, strictly speaking, paternalistic protective approaches. But that does not mean that the criminal law should be used to implement those reflections of paternalism.[81]

---

78 For the distinction between 'hard paternalism' and 'soft paternalism' see Joel Feinberg, *Harm to Self* (Oxford University Press, New York 1986) 12 et seq.

79 In Findlay, Odgers and Yeo, above n 21, 4, the authors, in relation to regulations on seat belts and helmets, state without further discussion: 'Paternalism is an inappropriate explanation here since we are concerned with individuals who should possess a sufficient degree of maturity to make their own decisions about the risks of such activities.' Such normative statements are very rare in the Australian literature. But in ruling out any legitimate criminalization based on paternalistic reasons so long as the concerned persons 'possess a sufficient degree of maturity', the authors do not discuss the principle at all, despite the extensive consequences this statement entails. Supporters of a paternalistic approach would argue that apparently the concerned individuals *cannot* 'make their own decisions about the risks of such activities' since the only reasonable decision would be to wear a seat belt/helmet. In other words, although it is not undisputed that paternalistic purposes are only legitimate if the concerned persons are lacking 'a sufficient degree of maturity', this statement simply ignores the discussion.

80 See, for example, McSherry and Naylor, above n 21, 200–202, mentioning paternalism, but then focusing on morality as a reason for criminalization; also see Bronitt and McSherry, above n 21, 532–537.

81 Interview with Brent Fisse (Sydney, 22 August 2007).

> The argument to the contrary is that the people who consent may be overborne. They cannot consent to being killed or to having gross grievous bodily harm inflicted upon them. Such consent is not proportional. The sexual pleasure may not then be proportional to the harm that is done to them and to others. That is a somewhat paternalistic approach. It smacks of 'nanny knows best'. The state may say to people, 'well you say you are getting pleasure out of this activity, we say you are not really giving true consent because this activity is not consentable.' I find that a difficult argument to swallow.[82]

> My own view is that if consent is genuinely and properly given to that kind of conduct, then it should not be criminalized. I think that people should be free to do with their own bodies what they choose to do, provided that it is not causing harm to somebody else.[83]

> [S]peaking about sexual conduct to which a consent is given and assuming that the consent is one that is freely given by a person who is competent to give it and is not in any way being oppressed in order to consent, I suppose, the justification is that the authority to consent to sexual activity with one's body is part of that freedom which gives human dignity even if the individual abuses it from time to time. I suppose you should say, even if the individual chooses to abuse it from time to time. But even then, the term 'abuse' is something, which is open for controversy.[84]

As mentioned, the *Rechtsgutstheorie* does not consider deliberate self-harm and harm that is inflicted with consent to justify criminalization. The same view is held by Feinberg.

While the interviews revealed that this is also the opinion of many Australian criminal lawyers, the Australian literature does not deal with paternalism as a general principle for criminalization at all.[85]

Republican Theories of Criminal Justice

In their criminal law text, Bronitt and McSherry give an introduction to republican theories of criminal justice and state that these also include a redefinition of 'the aims and the scope of the criminal law'.[86] They also argue that 'republicanism is a normative theory concerned with the promotion of positive social freedom (rather

---

82 Interview with Sir Michael Kirby (Sydney, 24 July 2007).

83 Interview with Nicolas Cowdery (Sydney, 13 August 2007).

84 Interview with Sir Gerard Brennan (Sydney, 15 August 2007).

85 The topic is brought up though when dealing with individual offences, for example, drug laws. See below p. 109 et seq.

86 Bronitt and McSherry, above n 21, 63.

than negative individual freedom)'[87] and connect this to the approach that aims to integrate the harm principle with the welfare principle mentioned above.

In contrast to the principles presented so far, republican theory does not directly set limits for criminalization. Instead, it is a broad theoretical approach to the criminal justice system as a whole. It argues that the promotion of the republican conception of liberty, called 'dominion', is the legitimate purpose of the criminal justice system. Although it also includes debates on 'the scope and type of criminal laws',[88] the main focus of this global approach is on questions surrounding policing, criminal process and sentencing. Regarding limits for criminalization, the general presumption in favour of parsimony, which is promoted by republican theory, only imposes the 'onus of proof … on those justifying any intervention'.[89] It does, however, not tell us which considerations are considered to validly prove the legitimacy of a criminal offence. The general notion that the whole criminal justice system ought to promote dominion is clearly not able to provide a useful criterion for determining the legitimacy of criminalization. Hence, even in the presentation of the theory by Bronitt and McSherry, no concrete offence is identified as one not considered legitimate according to republican theory.

Despite the fact that republican theory does not directly give answers to questions on the legitimate limits of criminalization, it is comparable to the *Rechtsgutstheorie* in its attempt to promote autonomy of the individual without neglecting the essential meaning of social and relational aspects of human life.

A Principle for Every Case

> The whole idea here is that you do not need to say we need one principle and one principle only to deal with all these situations. Principles have to be developed as cases come along.[90]

The most obvious difference between German *Rechtsgutstheorie* and the Australian perspective is the reference to only one criterion on the one hand and the consideration of several principles on the other. But this divergence, which might in itself be sufficient to describe the general contrast between the German- and the English-speaking approaches,[91] is only the first step to the understanding of the Australian perspective.

In addition to the fact that Australian scholars refer to several principles instead of just one criterion, this overview has shown two things. First, each of the principles presented is able to function as both a descriptive and a normative tool. They can provide answers to the question 'Why is something criminal?' as

87 Ibid., 62.
88 Ibid., 66.
89 Ibid., 65.
90 Interview with Dennis Baker (Sydney, 20 August 2007).
91 See Seher, above n 6, 45–46.

well as 'Is the criminalization legitimate?' Secondly, in the Australian discussion, the principles are not primarily used to establish legitimate limits of the criminal law – in a normative sense – but rather only to analyse reasons for criminalization – in a descriptive sense. Every principle invoked itself provides motives for criminalization. Combined, they cover every possible motivation for the state to prohibit behaviour. In this way, the entirety of the principles reflects the entirety of possible reasons for criminalization. Whether or not these reasons and the relevant principles are considered to be good reasons is not part, or at least not the focus, of the Australian discussion. In this descriptive capacity the principle-based approach differs sharply from the *Rechtsgutstheorie*. The German theory is neither designed nor used to describe *possible* reasons for criminalization. Its only function is to determine whether something is legitimately criminalized.

Thus, the Australian perspective not only differs from the German approach, which establishes one single criterion as a necessary condition for criminalization, but it also differs from the view that considers only some of the discussed principles to provide 'good reasons' to prohibit certain forms of behaviour, which is a view articulated in other English-speaking countries.

This approach, being more descriptive than normative, is a special feature of the Australian discussion. Why, in the Australian context, a set of limiting principles is primarily used in a descriptive way, will be analysed in the following section.

A Change Towards Theory

> In the past, many writers of texts on criminal law have tended to be obsessed with the issue of individual criminal responsibility. They have shown far less attention to developing general principles designed to limit the types of behaviour proscribed by criminal law. They have had little, if anything, to say about the subject matter of the criminal law and have quietly watched the gradual expansion of criminal law into areas of behaviour far beyond the scope of the common law crimes, including behaviour which is no more than preparatory to the causing of harmful consequences (e.g., possession of prohibited drugs), and behaviour which is arguably not harmful at all. This has been regarded as being beyond the brief of the study of criminal law.[92]

As we have seen, the content of the contemporary Australian discussion on the limits of criminal law is dominated by several principles. Further, these principles are not primarily considered in terms of their limiting function, but rather only in their explanatory dimension. In the course of the analysis it has been indicated that this approach is due to a general discrepancy between the ways in which the question on the limits of the criminal law is dealt with in Australia and Germany respectively.

---

92 Brown et al., above n 21, 12.

This section focuses on the formal structure of the discussion. The way in which the question is dealt with in Australia will be analysed as progressing from an originally atheoretical approach, which was typical of classic Australian criminal law texts, towards the criminological perspective that is dominant today.

The Classic Understanding: Application of the Law as it Stands

When going through the Australian textbooks on criminal law, one soon recognizes enormous differences from the German texts. Obviously, the common law tradition on the one hand and a civil law system on the other already provide for fundamental differences. Further, the fact that in Australia criminal law is (mainly) a state power,[93] while it is (almost entirely) a federal power in Germany,[94] leads to differences as well. Finally, the distinction between jurisdictions with a criminal code[95] and those without statutes that comprehensively lay down the criminal law[96] in Australia also influences the structure of Australian criminal law texts.[97] But, besides these differences regarding the sources of criminal law, another crucial discrepancy concerns the presentation of theory in general and the legitimate scope of the criminal law in particular. The classic Australian textbooks, like *Howard's Criminal Law*,[98] which was the basic Australian criminal law text for decades,[99] do not include statements on criminal law theory; they only deal with the application of the law as it stands.[100] Accordingly, generations of former Australian law students were not taught much, if anything, about criminal law theory in general, not to mention the legitimate scope of the criminal law in particular.

The only Australian textbook to explicitly mention and explain the phrase 'the limits of criminal law', is that of Brown et al. The authors also give a reason for the lack of a discussion on the topic, which is connected to the way in which the classic Australian criminal law texts – like *Howard's Criminal Law* – are structured:

---

93 See Australian Law Reform Commission, *Same Crime, Same Time: Sentencing of Federal Offenders, Report 103* (ALRC, Sydney 2006) 95.

94 See Roxin, *Allgemeiner Teil, Band I*, above n 36, 13.

95 The so-called 'code states' are Queensland, Tasmania, Western Australia, the Northern Territory and the Australian Capital Territory as well as the Commonwealth.

96 The so-called 'common law states' are New South Wales, South Australia and Victoria.

97 See, for example, Penny Crofts, *Essential Criminal Law*, Australian essential series (3rd edn Cavendish, Coogee 2005) 1–4.

98 Brent Fisse, *Howard's Criminal Law* (5th edn The Law Book Company Limited, Sydney 1990).

99 Interview with Matthew Goode (Adelaide, 14 August 2007).

100 Another classic text is Peter Gillies, *Criminal Law* (4th edn LBC Information Services, North Ryde 1997). This book contains a section that is headed 'Purposes of the Criminal Law' which is one and a half pages in length and states the aims of punishment.

> The neglect of the issue of the limits of the criminal law is at least in part attributable to the points made in the previous section – that criminal law has traditionally been constituted so as to include only those offences (homicide, assault, sexual assault, theft) in relation to which it is assumed that there is little disagreement, at least at a general level, as to the legitimacy of their place in criminal law.[101]

Further investigation into why the classic approach neglects these questions identified three primary reasons: historical, sceptical and pragmatic.

An English Tradition

> That is a good question and a hard one to answer. I think, partly, you have to go into the history of the academic teaching of law in Australia. I do not know much about Germany and Europe, but my guess is that through the much longer history there, law teaching is seen, historically, as having more links with the central general disciplines like philosophy. Whereas in Australia, law teaching was largely seen as being vocationally oriented. It was predominantly carried out by, in the early stages at least, practitioners. There was a pragmatic concern to teach the law as it was, not to question it. We are only, just now, in some senses, coming out of that kind of tradition. I think it is changing and hopefully our book will be one little part of helping to bring that change.
>
> But I really agree with the question. It is an interesting thing to think of: why is it that, in criminal law, of all places, there has been this incredible narrowness, this very, very vocationally oriented black letter law, unquestioning approach. You would think that if any area would open itself up to philosophical or sociological or empirical analysis, to the question of what are the limits and functions of law, it would be the criminal law. It is only from the early 1970s, in Australia, it is starting to happen. It is not just our book now. That sort of approach has been picked up now in a couple of other texts: the Bronitt/McSherry book does it and another one by McSherry. There is a type of more questioning book around today. But still, by and large, if you look at any of the traditional textbooks, as you said, now they have a chapter or a section, but only three or five or seven pages long and it is not substantial. There is a flavour of 'let us get this out of the way' rather than bother thinking about it more seriously.[102]

In relation to the historical argument, two different but interdependent points are emphasized: the common law tradition and the corresponding system of legal education. 'The common law tradition has traditionally been based on the solution

101 Brown et al., above n 21, 13.

102 Interview with David Brown (Sydney, 13 August 2007).

to discrete individual cases and not to the application of an overarching principle, which is then applied down with subsets which attract its operation.'[103]

> Now why does the common law not deal with such philosophical issues? The answer is simple. It is because the common law is made by the judges. The judges of the English tradition (including in Australia) tend to feel very uncomfortable about conceptual issues of broad generality. This may be because judges are generally former barristers. Retired barristers are people who, for 20 or so years, have spent their time fighting cases in court – real cases, affecting real people with real legal questions. Generally speaking, they have not got the time, inclination, energy or interest to sit there and ponder about conceptual questions: about what it is all about and why are we doing this? They simply go from precedent to precedent, solving problems.[104]

This common law tradition, which focuses on the just solution of individual cases without aiming for the rationalization of the system in total as is typical of Continental civil law systems, is also reflected in the legal education:

> It is an English-speaking phenomenon. I grew up in the United States. The traditional textbooks in criminal law that I would have used there, the same in the United Kingdom and I am sure the same in Canada, are very ahistorical, asocial and acultural. They are very much based on the case method, which is really the old British empiricist model. It is the opposite of the kind of rationalist approach you are talking about. They use it in business schools as well, saying here are case studies and you have to rationalize back or reason back. The whole legal tradition in English-speaking countries has been much more that apprenticeship or empiricist model. In Australia, until the late 1970s, the majority of Australian lawyers were trained through the apprenticeship model. It was only in the 70s that the university educated lawyers tipped the balance. And so we have not had the rationalist projects that you have had in Europe since the 1200s (at the University of Bologna etc). So there have been 700 years of that tradition in Continental Europe while the English tradition has been much more practice-based. The textbooks very much reflected that.[105]

While David Weisbrot regards this type of legal education to be an 'English-speaking phenomenon', another academic considered it to be particularly true for Australia:

> I also find a very low level of theoretical literacy, generally, which is to do with that law school 'trade school' mentality. A lot of people studied only law in

103 Interview with Sir Gerard Brennan (Sydney, 15 August 2007).
104 Interview with Sir Michael Kirby (Sydney, 24 July 2007).
105 Interview with David Weisbrot (Sydney, 12 September 2007).

> earlier times and they would not have studied legal theory. If they did, they hated it and it was an elective typically, until a recommendation of the Pearce Committee in 1989 made it compulsory. So, in Australia, legal theory never constituted formally a part of legal education, whereas there is a very strongly different tradition in the UK.[106]

This view is also shared by David Brown, co-author of one of the leading criminal law texts in New South Wales,[107] who also regards the classic system of legal education in Australia to be a reason for the lack of academic writing on the topic:

> I think it is very much tied up with the tradition of law teaching – quite literally. I did not do my degree here. I did it in Auckland in the late 1960s early 1970s. But from what I hear from people here, particularly at Sydney University, most of the law teachers were barristers and, in some cases judges, who taught at the end of the day and read out from notes that they had prepared, in some cases, 10, 15, 20 years ago. They just read them out and the set of notes would circulate and people would not have to go to the lectures. That is dreadful; incredibly unthinking. But clearly, legal education has been intellectualized in the last three decades or so.[108]

Disregarding the different opinions on whether this is an 'English-speaking phenomenon' or a particular Australian occurrence, most of the experts interviewed regard the common law tradition and the corresponding history of legal education to be a reason for the lack of academic discussion on the limits of criminal law in Australia.

General Scepticism Towards Theory The tradition of legal education described above inevitably produces, among lawyers educated in this system, scepticism towards theory in general and normative theories on the legitimate scope of the criminal law in particular.

> The second reason, I suppose, being intellectually acclimatized to the common law system, would be a profound scepticism about providing an overarching principle, which would have general application across the board to criminal offences and would therefore tend to mislead in the exposition of any of the particular provisions of the criminal law.[109]

106 Interview with a professor of law at an Australian university (30 August 2007).
107 Interview with Dennis Baker (Sydney, 20 August 2007).
108 Interview with David Brown (Sydney, 13 August 2007).
109 Interview with Sir Gerard Brennan (Sydney, 15 August 2007).

> However, ultimately, I think it is very, very difficult to find either any singular principle or, indeed, a set of principles that you can operate in any kind of rationalist way either to explain the content of the existing criminal law as we know it or to guide some ideal criminal law as we might wish it to be.[110]

This general scepticism towards theory and normative theorizing in particular is furthermore attributed to the legislative practice in Australia, which does not take a theoretical approach, but is also considered to be very pragmatic:

> There is not a lot of interest in attempting to formulate normative theories because of, when one looks at how the law develops, it is not the product of any normative theory, whether articulated or under the surface. Therefore, it is a fairly pointless exercise.[111]

> I think those kinds of 'process concerns'[112] are in some ways more useful, given, in response to other questions, what I call 'the unprincipled approach to criminal law', where essentially criminal law is enacted on the basis of whatever the political party in power thinks is in their legitimate interests or in the interest of dampening down concern about law and order as a political issue or whatever. In other words, it is a largely unprincipled exercise. I do not think that the solution to an unprincipled exercise is to come up with a set of philosophical principles because I do not think that is going to happen at a level of political reality. That is just not what is going to happen. But I do think we can come up with a set of process concerns that ought to be adopted.[113]

> There is scepticism towards theory and its value. I do not think it appeals to most students. I do not think it appeals to most judges and if it were it would be a very narrow range of judges. And, finally, I feel our legislature is very tied to a common sense politics of law and order that takes little account of the range of experts that might be available. They would take more notice of the criminologist than they would a criminal law theorist, which is due to a, generalizing, very strongly pragmatic stream in Australian culture that probably does not see the value of theory. And if you can achieve the same thing without framing it in theoretical terms it will be that much more compelling.[114]

---

110 Interview with David Brown (Sydney, 13 August 2007).

111 Interview with Stephen Odgers (Sydney, 27 August 2007).

112 David Brown refers to Lord Williams of Mostyn answering a parliamentary question in England. See Brown et al., above n 21, 20.

113 Interview with David Brown (Sydney, 13 August 2007).

114 Interview with a professor of law at an Australian university (30 August 2007).

Pragmatism: No Bill of Rights, So What is the Point? The described scepticism towards theory is also connected to another major characteristic of Australian legal scholarship, which can be described as pragmatism.

> But in the end what seems to be paramount is a very strong, and I see it in Australian culture generally, principle of pragmatism. I have never actually articulated this until your interview, but the more I think about it, it is there in a range of examples.[115]

The 'pragmatic reason' for the lack of discussion of the legitimate limits for criminalization among Australian scholars is actually a constitutional one. It invokes the lack of a bill of rights in Australia, which leads to the result that the High Court of Australia (in this regard the equivalent to the Federal Constitutional Court in Germany) has, as far as can be seen, not even had to decide a single case concerning the legitimate limits of the substantive criminal law in terms of its content.[116]

> Because they [Canada] have a Bill of Rights as well, it puts them in a different position to Australia where there are no constitutional human rights – or barely none. That also would explain, I suppose, why the High Court of Australia has not got involved in a lot of this stuff. You see it in Europe, in America and in Canada, but you do not see it here.[117]

Therefore, judgments of Australian courts, especially by the High Court, do not provide relevant information on the topic.

The argument that this fact also hinders academic discussion on the topic goes like this: if, in the end, a criminal offence cannot be successfully challenged before the courts because there is no bill of rights against which the offence can be measured, the whole discussion on legitimate limits of the criminal law is pointless, as it does not have any practical influence.

> There is not any constitutional limitation, as I have explained to you, so you do not get great academic judgements, like you do in Canada, for example, about the limits of the criminal law measured against a bill of rights. It is possible

115 Ibid.

116 A different question to be answered by the courts is whether the common law can still 'produce' new criminal offences. This problem is different because it concerns the legitimate procedure for making law in light of the separation of powers doctrine, but not the actual content of the laws. Another case sometimes referred to in this context is *Kable v DPP* (NSW) (1996) 189 CLR 51. However, *Kable* only concerns questions about individual case legislation in the field of preventive detention and not the legitimate content of substantive criminal law. See Brown et al., above n 21, 257–261.

117 Interview with Dennis Baker (Sydney, 20 August 2007).

> to do all sorts of stuff in Canada, based on some interesting Supreme Court of Canada opinions, and it is done. Canada has a burgeoning judicial, academic and conference discussion about these things as a result.
>
> There is no point to it here! Why would you do it?[118]

This point, as well as the equally pragmatic argument that legislative practice disregards theoretical considerations, can probably only be understood in the context of the common law tradition. For a Continental jurist, the absence of a theory's application by the legislature or the courts is not regarded to be a hindrance for academic discussion and support for the theory. By contrast, it is a particular characteristic of legal theories that they are applied 'in theory' but not necessarily also 'in practice'. Whether or not the legislature itself or the courts that have the power to control the legislature's decisions apply such theories, neither says anything about a particular theory's legitimacy nor about the value of such theories in general. In other words: normative theories do not depend on their application in practice. By contrast, influencing practice is a *goal* of normative theorizing – not a *requirement*. This understanding is well demonstrated by the fact that the *Rechtsgutstheorie* is most influential in the German discussion, despite the fact that it has not been adopted by the Federal Constitutional Court. Ultimately, as the examples of the criminal law reform in Germany of the 1960s and 1970s and the dissenting judicial opinion of Hassemer in the recent judgment on incest show, academic discussion of theory and its place as part of every law student's education can eventually influence practice – even though it might take a long time. But normative legal theories can never influence practice straight away – they do not have automatic application. In order to influence practice, they have to be applied by practitioners. This requires a mature legal culture that considers theory to be important and valid, so that generations of lawyers are taught theories at law school before they may eventually influence practice – as judges, members of parliament, members of committees and law reform commissions, etc.

The New Approach – Theory Overload?

The 'intellectualization of legal education' mentioned by David Brown is also reflected in the new approaches taken by some of the contemporary criminal law textbooks. In contrast to the classic approach, represented by *Howard's Criminal Law* which focused only on the practical application of the law, these newer texts also contain large sections dealing with criminal law theory.[119]

---

118 Interview with Matthew Goode (Adelaide, 14 August 2007).

119 For example Brown et al., above n 21, Chapters 1 and 2; Bronitt and McSherry, above n 21, Part 1; also see L. Waller and C.R. Williams, *Criminal Law: Texts and Cases* (10th edn LexisNexis Butterworths, Chatswood 2005), Part 1; McSherry and Naylor, above n 21, Part 1.

David Brown described this new approach of Australian criminal law texts as being 'more questioning', and, indeed, these newer books that include whole chapters or large sections on theory raise a lot of questions, for example, questions on the general benefits of theory,[120] on the aims of the criminal law[121] and on criminalization.[122]

However, the differences between the way in which theory is dealt with in the German and Australian texts are enormous. They concern the general understanding of the scope of the term theory (Criminology versus Jurisprudence – Criminalization versus Limits of Criminal Law) and, following from that, the way in which theoretical considerations are presented in the texts (Descriptive versus Normative).

Criminology versus Jurisprudence – Criminalization versus Limits of Criminal Law

> Criminal law theory, how sophisticated is it? In traditional terms, criminal law theory in Australia has largely drifted down a criminal justice and criminological route, much more than an analytical jurisprudence model. By that I mean that there is a lot less thinking about issues around criminalization by Australian scholars than broader criminological questions. The short answer is, I do not think academics have done a huge amount, normatively, to rethink the criminal law. And the criminal justice scholars that have made a contribution have made a contribution to restorative justice, to regulation (criminal law seen at a regulatory spectrum). But in terms of core theories: not much. The short answer: I do not think the academics have done much.[123]

The first difference to the way in which theory is included in German criminal law texts is fundamental. It is based on a differing understanding and treatment of the terms jurisprudence, criminal law theory and criminology.

In Germany, there is no articulated distinction between the study of criminal law and criminal law theory in the way it is emphasized in Australia. First of all, there is no discussion of the general value of criminal law theory in standard German textbooks. Theory is not seen as an area that needed somehow to be included in criminal law texts because it is already regarded as a basic part of the study of criminal law.

The difference between the German approach and that of the Australian texts, which deal with theory in a separate section and treat it as something different from the normal study of criminal law, is not only due to the different history of treatment of this topic, but also a different understanding of the term theory.

---

120 For example Bronitt and McSherry, above n 21, 3–6.

121 For example Waller and Williams, above n 119, 16–21.

122 For example Brown et al., above n 21, 39–119.

123 Interview with a professor of law at an Australian university (30 August 2007).

The German understanding of criminal law theory is analytic and normative. Questions on how the criminal law does operate and how it should operate are asked and answered. The normative element of such thinking is the crucial quality of criminal law theory. In Australian terms, this approach would be called jurisprudential. On the other hand, most of the German criminal law texts do not discuss criminological aspects as criminology is considered to be a discipline related to, but not incorporated into, the study of criminal law.[124] On the other hand, criminal law theory, in the analytic, normative, jurisprudential sense described, is not regarded as a separate discipline, but rather as a part of the study of criminal law.

While criminal law theory deals with questions about the *law* (how it works and how it should work) and uses analytical and normative, legal and philosophical approaches, criminology deals with questions about the *reality* of crime using sociological, psychological and, particularly, empirical analysis.[125] The Australian texts that deal with theory, on the other hand, do not make a distinction between criminal law theory and criminology – both are regarded to be part of a broader category, called theory, which itself is, historically, not considered to be part of the general study of criminal law.

In summary, the crucial difference can be described as follows: in Germany, questions about the legitimate scope of the criminal law are regarded to be part of criminal law theory, which itself is considered to be part of the general study of criminal law. This is a jurisprudential approach to the criminal law curriculum. In Australia, these questions on the limits of criminal law are also considered to be theoretical. But criminal law theory, in contrast to Germany, is not regarded as belonging to the general study of criminal law, but to a separate category called theory which also, and mainly, includes criminological issues. The main distinction can therefore be described in terms of the differing emphasis on jurisprudence and criminology respectively.

A good example of this difference is a question dealt with in many new Australian criminal law texts, but not in the German ones: 'What is a crime?'[126] In Australia, this question is usually answered as follows: first, the 'formal' answer given by Glanville Williams[127] is presented: 'A crime (or offence) is a legal wrong that can be followed by criminal proceedings which may result in punishment.'[128] This definition is then usually criticized for its positivistic approach and for neglecting

124 While criminal law is a compulsory subject, criminology is an elective course.

125 See, for example, Roxin, *Allgemeiner Teil, Band I*, above n 36, 6.

126 See, for example, McSherry and Naylor, above n 21, 3–17; Brown et al., above n 21, 44–45; see also Bronitt and McSherry, above n 21, 6–10.

127 Glanville Williams, *Textbook of Criminal Law* (2nd edn Stevens & Sons, London 1983) 27.

128 See, for example, Bronitt and McSherry, above n 21, 6; McSherry and Naylor, above n 21, 5; Brown et al., above n 21, 44–45.

the reality of crime.[129] Finally, different critical, criminological definitions of crime are presented.[130]

These differing perspectives on the definition of crime are not foreign to the German discussion. What is different, though, is the way they are dealt with in a criminal law textbook and accordingly in criminal law education. The critical approaches described in the Australian texts, are, in Germany, only presented in depth in criminology courses or texts. For the purposes of criminal law theory, understood in the jurisprudential sense, the formal answer, that the criminal law itself defines what a crime is, is sufficient.[131] As such, the criminal law as it stands becomes the subject of theorizing, and questions of whether everything that *is made* a crime by the state *should be* a crime can be dealt with. From a criminological perspective, on the other hand, there are many different legitimate answers to the question: 'What is a crime?' The question itself becomes the subject of theorizing – but not the normative question of what *should* be made a crime by the state.

In other words, the German, jurisprudential understanding of criminal law theory concerns normative questions on what the law should be. The definition of crime is therefore required simply to state which behaviour is currently considered criminal under the law. For criminology, on the other hand, it is essential at this early stage to question the legal definition of crime, as this approach deals with the reality of crime, criminals, punishment, etc.

Basic criminal law theory, in contrast to criminology, is considered to be part of the study of criminal law in Germany because it is also important for correct statutory interpretation. Theoretical knowledge is regarded as essential for the understanding and application of the criminal law. It is not seen as a different discipline, but as a necessary tool for the correct solution of problems in the field of criminal law.

The connection between theory and application of criminal law can be easily understood by considering the *Rechtsgutstheorie* as an example. One of the fundamental rules of statutory interpretation in German criminal law is that an offence be interpreted in consideration of its protected *Rechtsgut*. As the German criminal code does not explicitly state the protected *Rechtsgut* for every individual offence, a person interpreting the law must have basic knowledge of the *Rechtsgutstheorie* in order to first identify the protected *Rechtsgut*. As such, criminal law theory is tied in with the practical application of the criminal law, and a typical textbook will not even distinguish between theory and 'not theory', but only between different opinions formulated by scholars and the courts about what the protected *Rechtsgut* in relation to a particular offence is.

---

129 See, in particular, McSherry and Naylor, above n 21, 5; also see Brown et al., above n 21, 45.

130 See, in particular, McSherry and Naylor, above n 21, 6–16.

131 See also Bronitt and McSherry, above n 21, 7.

In Australia, on the other hand, some of the newer criminal law textbooks start with a whole chapter that deals only with theory.[132] Criminal law theory is presented as a discipline that is distinct from actual criminal law. And although these authors regard theory as beneficial for the study and understanding of criminal law, they also state that '[s]tudents, teachers and practitioners may legitimately question the value of theoretical perspectives on the criminal law. After all, competent legal analysis and a lifetime of criminal practice may be undertaken without any conscious intrusion of theory.'[133]

This difference between the Australian and the German understanding, which indeed does regard basic knowledge of criminal law theory as essential for competent legal analysis, again lies in the understanding of what is meant by 'theoretical perspectives on the criminal law'.

The Australian texts that include chapters on theory attempt to be most comprehensive by including every possible aspect of theory on the criminal law. As it says on the back of Bronitt and McSherry's text, '[t]he disciplines drawn on include criminology, feminism, legal history, human rights, sociology and psychology.'[134]

This approach of combining several disciplines in order to provide the most comprehensive picture is used particularly when dealing with questions of criminalization. Indeed, the term criminalization itself is considered to imply this multidisciplinary approach. In Brown et al.,[135] Nicola Lacey is quoted:

> [T]he term 'criminalization' constitutes an appropriate conceptual framework within which to gather together the constellation of social practices which form the subject matter of criminal law on the one hand and criminal justice and criminological studies on the other. Escaping the notion of crimes as 'given', the idea of criminalization captures the dynamic nature of the field as a set of interlocking practices in which the moments of 'defining' and 'responding to' can rarely be completely distinguished and in which legal and social (extra-legal) constructions of crime constantly interact. It accommodates the full range of relevant institutions within which those practices take shape and the disciplines which might be brought to bear on their analysis; it allows the instrumental and symbolic aspects of the field to be addressed, as well as encompassing empirical, interpretive and normative projects. It embraces questions about offenders and victims, individuals and collectivities, state and society.
>
> Within the framework of criminalization, we may therefore accommodate the relevant practices of a variety of social actors and institutions: citizens, the media, the police, prosecution agencies, courts, judges and lawyers, social workers, probation officers and those working in the penal and mental health systems,

132 See, for example, Bronitt and McSherry, above n 21, Part 1.

133 Bronitt and McSherry, Ibid., 67–68.

134 Ibid.

135 Brown et al., above n 21, 39–40.

> legislators and key members of the executive. We are also able to acknowledge the relevance of a wide variety of disciplines to the analysis of these institutions: sociology, psychology, political science, economics, legal studies, moral and political philosophy, and anthropology, to name only the most obvious. This we can do without collapsing the study of criminalization into a chaotic mass which escapes rigorous analysis, and without falling prey to fantasies about the possibility of a unitary synthesis of different approaches.[136]

In Germany, the term criminalization, or an equivalent synonym, is not used in this context. Instead, the question on the limits of criminal law is given a lot of attention. This is a perfect demonstration of the fundamental differences in the way that theory is dealt with in German and in Australian criminal law texts. In Australia, normative questions on the limits of criminal law are part of the broader theme of criminalization, which also includes all the other disciplines, views and methods mentioned by Nicola Lacey. As such, there is no clear distinction between criminology and criminal law theory as is typical in the German discussion. Instead, the term criminalization provides a large pool of different disciplines, theories and methodologies, and the question about the limits of criminal law is dealt with by using every available discipline from this pool. Accordingly, the chapters on theory in the newer Australian criminal law texts cover a wide variety of approaches which have in common only that they are theoretical rather than non-theoretical and differ both with respect to the discipline they belong to and the methodology they use.

> Posing the issues in terms of *criminalization* involves us from the start in *contextualising* criminal law. This entails ranging across traditional disciplinary boundaries and, in particular, bringing criminological and criminal justice perspectives to bear on the study of criminal law and the forces and conditions of its creation and development.[137]

The contextualizing and the 'ranging across traditional disciplinary boundaries' inevitably leads to the described mixture of criminal law theory and criminology.

> What kinds of behaviour are caught up within the criminal law? This is a question about the current content of the criminal law. But it soon leads to another question: What should be the content of the criminal law? In this chapter we will move backwards and forwards between those two questions about the phenomenon of crime: What *is* criminal? What *ought* to be criminal? And what factors affect the processes of *criminalization*?

---

136 Nicola Lacey, 'Legal Constructions of Crime' in Mike Maguire, Rod Morgan and Robert Reiner (eds), *The Oxford Handbook of Criminology* (3rd edn Oxford University Press, Oxford, New York 2002) 282.

137 Brown et al., above n 21, 39.

> The materials we have extracted respond to these questions from a variety of perspectives. Some of them differ sharply. Some of them focus on the nature of the behaviour defined as criminal, attempting to identify something in the essence of such behaviour which makes it criminal. By contrast, other approaches claim that the social response is the crucial factor, that essentially similar behaviour is perceived and treated differently by the social audience for reasons external to the behaviour itself. These factors might have to do with factors like changing historical circumstances, the social class of the perpetrator, the needs or fears of the social group.[138]

This incorporation of normative criminal law theory into a broader criminological framework is foreign to the German discussion. The key to the understanding of this major difference is provided by the term jurisprudence. In Australia, jurisprudence is considered to be a special discipline, 'basically philosophy of law',[139] which is related but not necessarily essential to the successful study and practice of law. Jurisprudence is therefore not compulsory as an undergraduate subject in Australia. In Germany, the subject of study itself, which is called law in English-speaking countries, is called *Jurisprudenz* or *Rechtswissenschaf*, which literally translates as 'legal science'. According to this, the study of law (or legal science) not only includes the application of law – although this is the major part – but also the scientific analysis of the origin, the development and the function of the law.

This is not to say that every German law graduate is an expert in these fields. Rather, because the qualifying examination is governed by the states and not the universities and therefore generally only requires the students to apply the law to a (hypothetical) case, the majority of law students focus on this area too. Nevertheless, legal education at German universities and, correspondingly, the law textbooks aim to take a jurisprudential approach to law rather than presenting it in a practice-focused manner.[140]

This explains why, on the one hand, the German criminal law texts are more theoretical (jurisprudential) than the classic Australian texts, while, on the other hand, they do not cover as many theoretical (criminological) approaches as the modern Australian textbooks do.

In summary: the classic Australian criminal law text is atheoretical and deals only with the application of the law as it stands; the typical German textbook is jurisprudential, and it also deals with normative questions about how the law should be; finally, the newer Australian textbooks are criminological, and draw on

138 Ibid.

139 Interview with Dennis Baker (Sydney, 20 August 2007).

140 This theoretical education at German law schools also leads to the great majority of law students paying a private coach for at least one year before sitting the First State Exam in order to be prepared for the rather practice-focused exam.

a wide variety of disciplines to include 'theoretical perspectives on the criminal law'.

Normative versus Descriptive 'Indeed, the unconscious slippage from the "is" to the "ought" is a powerful rhetorical strategy of legal persuasion used by lawyers, judges and academics alike.'[141]

The second difference, which results from the first one, is the way in which questions concerning theory are presented and answered. As shown in Chapter 2, the typical German text on the general part of the criminal law will not only *present* different normative theories, but also *make* normative statements on the legitimate function and limits of the criminal law. The authors will demonstrate and defend their opinion on the issue, references to similar and dissenting opinions will be given and arguments for their view as well as for and against other views will be provided. In this manner, the authors try to convince the reader of their opinion, while also presenting alternative views and arguments.

On the other hand, in the Australian texts that deal with the topic, normative statements are generally avoided. While different (normative) views are *presented*, the authors themselves do not take a firm stand and defend one opinion, but rather try to be as descriptive as possible. They do not attempt to say which (normative) approach they think is right, but rather describe which view is most capable of explaining the existence of certain offences. In this way, the normative character of the opinions presented is blurred and the 'slippage from the "is" to the "ought"', mentioned in the quotation above, becomes, in turn, applicable to the discussion of normative theories: the law as it stands is not *criticized* by using a particular concept, but the offences are *explained* by using several different, actually normative concepts.

In other words, while the German authors present the discussion by arguing for their own point of view and then criticize offences that do not fit within their concept, the Australians describe many different opinions as neutrally as possible and use all of them to give reasons for the criminalization of certain forms of behaviour – not to criticize it.[142]

More Descriptive than Critical = More Pragmatic than Dogmatic = More Political than Legal

The two different levels analysed in this chapter – the material and the formal – interact with each other. The way in which the question of legitimate limits of the criminal law is dealt with in Australia, as well as the actual content of

141 Bronitt and McSherry, above n 21, 51.

142 See, for example, Bronitt and McSherry, above n 21, 51: 'To provide resources for normative reconstruction, this section provides an overview of some significant theories'; Brown et al., above n 21, 39: 'The materials we have extracted respond to these questions from a variety of perspectives. Some of them differ sharply.'

the discussion, differ from both the German approach and the English-speaking approaches of the United States and the United Kingdom.

Today, Australian criminal law texts include large sections on theoretical views of the criminal law. As we have seen, the basic characteristic of the Australian discussion is its descriptive nature. The availability of several principles that are all treated as – more or less – legitimate leads to very pragmatic usage of these principles. One does not have to decide whether a principle in general is legitimate, but only whether it provides good reasons in a particular case. In this way, any discussion of legitimate limits of the criminal law is held not dogmatically, but pragmatically.

Finally, this way of dealing with criminal law as a subject influences the role of lawyers, in general, and legal academics, in particular, in the discussion. The issue is treated more as a 'political exercise'[143] than as a legal one. 'I think they [academics] are probably just reflecting what the political reality is. There is no political interest in that kind of dialogue.'[144]

> On the other hand, I think that is an inadequate response because if academics and to an extent judges are not going to be raising the question of limits, well then, who is? We cannot look to politicians to do so because they do not see it in their interest. They want to use the criminal law as a political weapon whenever they can. That is what they do. Therefore, it is up to judges and academics and lawyers and law reform commissions and so on to raise a way of thinking about the criminal law as a, what I have called 'limited resource'.[145]

Jurisprudential Benefits: Legal Argumentation

> Here, a restrictive concept of 'science' leads to jurists surrendering to legislative arbitrariness. Of course, criminal policy itself is not yet a science. But the development of limits for the content of criminal legislation, deduced from the requirements regarding criminal policy demanded by a liberal constitutional order governed by the rule of law, indeed belongs to the scientific tasks of jurisprudence.[146]

The differences between the Australian and the German approaches to criminal law theory described above have a major influence on the actual role of lawyers in the debate on the limits of criminal law. The criminological approach taken

143 Interview with Stephen Odgers (Sydney, 27 August 2007); interview with Ian Leader-Elliott (Adelaide, 14 August 2007); interview with Matthew Goode (Adelaide, 14 August 2007); Interview with David Brown (Sydney, 13 August 2007).

144 Interview with Brent Fisse (Sydney, 22 August 2007).

145 Interview with David Brown (Sydney, 13 August 2007).

146 Roxin, *Allgemeiner Teil, Band I*, above n 36, 50.

by Australian academics, which tries to consider as many different theoretical perspectives as possible to throw light on the criminal law, has the advantage of providing a most comprehensive picture. In this way, students (and future lawyers) learn more about the reality of crime and punishment, the problems the criminal law faces and even about the issues that affect the process of criminalization. This approach therefore provides a critical understanding of the criminal law.

But this strategy also has a fundamental flaw: Australian criminal lawyers cannot refer to an established concept in order to critique legislative decisions. Instead, they can refer to several different disciplines, pick what supports their argument and skip what opposes it, while others will simply invoke a different approach that supports their view. The problem is that, since they were developed in disciplines other than law, these different theories are never considered to produce legal arguments. Hence, many Australian lawyers consider it not to be their function to engage in discussions on criminal policy.

> I am very reluctant to express personal opinions. Not because I am really embarrassed about my own personal opinion and it would be an interesting 'coffee discussion' for me talking to a friend. I would express opinions, but I just question the value of me, in this context as a putative criminal law expert, saying anything.
>
> Can I say that I personally have written articles challenging the very role of academics in expressing opinions on those kinds of questions and challenging their expertise to be able to say anything about these things because it seems to me that these are questions about moral philosophy and sociology and politics that lawyers do not really have expertise in. Anybody is entitled to express their views about these questions. We are all moral creatures. But why is my opinion more valuable than anybody else's? I just query that.[147]

A main reason that German criminal lawyers, on the other hand, consider it to be their function to engage in questions about the legitimate limits of the criminal law is the jurisprudential structure of the *Rechtsgutstheorie* – its legal argumentation. The basic and most fundamental legal skill – independent of a common law or a civil law system – is the application of legal norms to individual cases. In Germany, the Latin-derived term 'subsumption' is used to describe this technique. The correct subsumption of an event in reality (the case) under a legal norm (the law) requires a definition of the terms of the norm as a first step. For example, in order to subsume the intentional killing of a loved one to save them from the agony of a terminal illness under the crime of murder[148] one needs first

147 Interview with Stephen Odgers (Sydney, 27 August 2007). One of the articles he is referring to is Stephen Odgers, 'Book Review. Principles of Criminal Law by Simon Bronitt and Bernadette McSherry. LBC Infomation Services 2001' (2001) Summer 2001/2002 *NSW Bar News* 66.

148 See Waller and Williams, above n 119, 24.

to have a definition of murder. Whatever the definition of murder might be in any given jurisdiction, it will be expressed in terms which themselves need to be clarified – defined – as well. That is the fundamental structure of legal work – the legal methodology. The *Rechtsgutstheorie* adopts this methodology by establishing a norm ('every criminal offence must protect a *Rechtsgut*'), defining the terms of this norm (for example, 'a *Rechtsgut* is a fact or established goal that is necessary for the free personality development of the individual, the realization of his or her civil rights and the functioning of a political system, which is based on these objectives'[149]) and then subsuming a particular offence (for example, murder) under this definition. The result will be that the offence of murder protects the *Rechtsgut* human life. This is a legitimate *Rechtsgut* because it is essential for the free personality development of the individual. Therefore, the criminalization of murder is considered to be legitimate.

In this way, the question of whether a particular behaviour is legitimately criminalized can be answered by applying a legal methodology. The obvious difference to the 'normal' legal subsumption is the fact that the norm which is to be applied is not a law, but a theory. Also, the facts that are to be subsumed under the norm are not taken from human conduct, but from laws. Nevertheless, independent of these differences concerning the sources of the norm and the facts, the crucial point is the legal methodology applied: norm – definition – subsumption.

It is not the intention here to glorify the *Rechtsgutstheorie* in general or to present it as the correct solution for the problem. However, what can be determined is that the way the concept operates gives lawyers familiar terrain for argumentation and it is therefore attractive to them. Because of this, German criminal lawyers do not hesitate to critique legislative decisions and the academic discussion – despite different points of view that lead to different definitions and subsumptions – is very extensive. The *Rechtsgutstheorie* does not always deliver clear and generally accepted answers, but it provides lawyers with a structure for a reasonable and scientific discussion on the legitimate scope of the criminal law, which can be applied to determine the legitimacy of individual offences. It provides a framework, a matrix for the discussion.

The lack of such a concept cast in legal terms and methodology is probably the reason Australian lawyers do not consider questions of criminal policy to belong to their expertise and function. The recent 'change towards theory' in the Australian criminal law texts cannot alter this because it is only broadening the spectrum of perspectives on the criminal law. Because it is introducing many different disciplines to the topic, it is not able to provide lawyers with a familiar line of argumentation. This is not to say that external views on the criminal law, which are introduced by the newer Australian textbooks, are not important for the discussion. By contrast, it would be desirable for the German scholarship to include more criminological views into the study of criminal law. However, it is argued that this

149 Roxin, *Allgemeiner Teil, Band I*, above n 36, 16.

way of theorizing does not provide a structure for legal argumentation in the way the *Rechtsgutstheorie* does.

A good example of the benefits of such a concept can be seen in relation to the so called 'law and order policy'[150] in Australia. While there is a lot of criticism of the legislative practice of reacting to certain incidents by enacting new 'one case statutes'[151] in Australia, this phenomenon is not foreign to Germany either. There, it is described by the term 'symbolic legislation'.[152] The difference between the Australian and the German criticism of such new offences is that the *Rechtsgutstheorie* provides German academics with a tool for argumentation. By analysing whether such offences are actually necessary to protect certain *Rechtsgüter* or whether they are just political responses to current cases that do not add anything to the protection of legal goods/interests, German lawyers can distinguish between legitimate offences and merely symbolic legislation. Australian scholars, on the other hand, do not have such a general concept to base their criticism on, which obviously makes it much harder for them to articulate their critique. If you do not have a clear and recognized concept for the determination of legitimate offences, you will inevitably also have problems convincing anyone of the illegitimacy of a particular offence.

150 Interview with a professor of law at an Australian university (30 August 2007).

151 Interview with Matthew Goode (Adelaide, 14 August 2007).

152 See above p. 14–15.

Chapter 5
Incest, Bestiality and Drugs – Legitimately Criminalized?

> The logic of prohibition is rarely subject to wider scrutiny, and fundamental questions about the legitimacy of criminalization are often deemed 'political' and therefore beyond the scope of the reform enterprise.[1]

> [I]ncest, basically, does not harm anyone if the parties are consenting; corpse bashing causes great offence but does not harm anyone if the person is dead and has no family and no one cares about the person. But would we ever see these acts decriminalized? Probably not.[2]

The 'normative flaw' in the descriptive approach dominant in the Australian discussion becomes apparent when looking at particular offences. The interviews revealed that there are strong concerns shared by many Australian criminal lawyers regarding the legitimacy of individual offences. But despite agreement that these offences should be rejected, the lack of a general normative concept for critique also influences the articulation of normative criticism in particular cases. There is no common normative ground to which the critique could refer. Further, even when expressing criticism of a particular offence, some interviewees still invoked 'political reality' as a hindrance to normative critique, while others focused more on the historical explanation for certain prohibitions rather than making normative statements.

In order to analyse the gap between the descriptive nature of the literature and the normative opinions presented in the interviews, this chapter presents three criminal offences, all of which are contested by the *Rechtsgutstheorie*, as examples: incest, which is a criminal offence in Germany as well as in every Australian jurisdiction; bestiality, which is a crime in Australia but was decriminalized in Germany in 1969; and the possession of illicit drugs for the purpose of self-administration, which, again, is criminal in both countries.[3]

It will be argued that despite the fact that the offences are commonly rejected, lack of agreement on a general normative concept poses a problem for the articulation of normative critique in relation to particular cases as well.

---

1 Simon Bronitt and Bernadette McSherry, *Principles of Criminal Law* (2nd edn Thomson Lawbook, Pyrmont 2005) 786.

2 Interview with Dennis Baker (Sydney, 20 August 2007).

3 Possession is used here because the actual self-administration is criminal in Australia, but not in Germany.

Incest

Both in Australia and Germany, sexual intercourse between consenting adult relatives is criminalized as incest.[4] In both countries, recent incest cases have attracted wide-scale media coverage.

In Germany, there was the case of brother and sister who met for the first time aged 24 and 16 years respectively. They fell in love, lived together and had four children. Several convictions for incest against the brother finally led to the judgement of the Federal Constitutional Court, discussed above in Chapter 2, in which the offence was held to be constitutional.[5]

In Australia, a father and daughter aged 31 met after 30 years' separation. They formed a relationship and had two children together. The first child died within days of birth. On 20 March 2008, the couple were sentenced to a three-year good behaviour bond after pleading guilty to two counts of performing an act of incest. At sentencing, the presiding judge said: 'Relevant factors include: the need to prevent the high risk of congenital defects of children born of incestuous relationships; and to prevent children, who are brought up in a family unit founded on an incestuous relationship, suffering psychological harm and social stigmatization.'[6]

It is important to make clear, because the term 'incest' does not provide a distinction, that both cases referred to above are different to the recently revealed Austrian case of long-lasting sexual abuse of a daughter by her father. This horrifying case is about rape, deprivation of liberty and other offences which were all committed against the victim's will. These issues are not relevant to the discussion of the legitimacy of the offence of incest, which concerns only consensual activities between adults.

While the *Rechtsgutstheorie* does not consider any of the reasons in favour of criminalization discussed above to legitimate criminalization, the majority of the Federal Constitutional Court regarded the 'aggregation of comprehensible purposes for punishment, also taking into consideration the historico-culturally-based and still influential public opinion that incest is worthy of being punished, which can also be detected in the international comparison',[7] to provide a constitutional ground for criminalization. In other words: '[w]ith the offence challenged here, the legislature pursues goals which are not constitutionally objectionable and which,

4 There are differences regarding the degree of familial relationship required for the offence both amongst the different Australian jurisdictions and in Germany. The crucial communality is that in every Australian jurisdiction and in Germany, consensual sexual intercourse between adult relatives is criminalized.

5 For a detailed description of the history of the case see BVerfG, NJW 2008, 1137.

6 Staff Writers, www.news.com.au, Incest couple John and Jenny Deaves's first child died (7 April 2008) <http://www.news.com.au/story/0,23599,23494953-2,00.html> accessed 19 June 2009.

7 BVerfG, NJW 2008, 1137, 1140.

at least in combination, legitimate a constraint to the general right of personality.'[8] The 'aggregation of comprehensible purposes of punishment' referred to by the court is to be rejected in terms of the *Rechtsgutstheorie* because the combination of several reasons that are not considered to be sufficient on their own does not provide a sufficient reason – not even 'at least in combination'.[9]

In Australia, the Model Criminal Code Officers Committee (MCCOC) proposed that the 'criminal offence of incest between consenting adults should be abolished'.[10] This suggestion was widely misinterpreted as meaning the Committee had recommended the 'abolition of the law which criminalizes sexual contact between adults and related *children*.'[11] Besides this critique, which was based on an incorrect interpretation of the proposition, there was also opposition based on two other arguments (referring to consideration of remote harms and public morality): the risk of inbreeding and the 'idea that the criminal law should reflect sexual practices thought to be distasteful or contrary to particular religious conviction by the enactment of a serious criminal offence'.[12] The only argument in favour of criminalization the Committee considered that 'might have made any sense, was the argument that adults who have sexually abused children in the past continue the sexual relationship after the child has passed the age of consent'.[13] Finally, 'the Committee was compelled to change its mind by the forces of darkness and ignorance. It recommended an offence of incest.'[14]

The question of the legitimacy of the offence of incest in Australia provides a perfect example of the problems that the lack of a general normative concept creates. The criminalization of incest could theoretically be reasoned by several, if not all, of the discussed principles. First of all, the acknowledgement of morality as a ground for criminalization easily provides a reason for the prohibition of incest. Related to that, the offence principle could provide a good reason for criminalization as incest is a social taboo that is generally considered to be repulsive. Furthermore, the consideration of remote and indirect harms could legitimate the offence as children that are born from incestuous relationships might have an increased risk of genetic defects and will also face psychological and social difficulties. The welfare principle could provide a reason for criminalization as it is arguable that society as

8 BVerfG, NJW 1137, 1139.

9 For this criticism see Roland Hefendehl, *Inzestverbot: BVerfG nimmt sich Auszeit und erklärt sich für das Strafrecht nicht für zuständig* (15 March 2008) <http://www.smartnuts.com/index.php/main/inzestverbot_bverfg_nimmt_sich_eine_auszeit_uun_erklaert_sich_fuer_das_stra/> accessed 19 June 2009; Tatjana Hörnle, 'Das Verbot des Geschwisterinzests – Verfassungsgerichtliche Bestätigung und verfassungsrechtliche Kritik' (2008) *NJW* 2085, 2088.

10 M.R. Goode, 'Constructing Criminal Law Reform and the Model Criminal Code' (2002) 26 *Criminal Law Journal* 152, 161.

11 Ibid.

12 Ibid.

13 Ibid., 162.

14 Ibid., 163.

a whole is better off without having to deal with incestuous relationships. Finally, the public interest seems to be in favour of criminalization.

In the Australian textbooks, the offence of incest is discussed within the framework of 'sexual offences involving children'.[15] Interestingly, the focus is not on the fact that the offence also includes sexual conduct between consenting relatives who are adults. While, in the texts, the existence of the offence is historically explained as the reinforcement of 'the moral and religious taboo against consanguinity'[16] or the aim to 'prevent inbreeding',[17] the contemporary explanation is seen in the protection of children against sexual abuse within the family.[18] None of the Australian texts argues that the offence is illegitimate. In contrast, where a statement is made, it is said that 'the arguments for and against the retention of the crime of incest are finely balanced.'[19]

In favour of criminalization, it is further argued that 'there may be practical advantages in having an overlap in statutory offences in relation to sexual abuse of children and young persons, particularly because of the problematic nature of proving non-consent to sexual intercourse for the offences of rape and indecent assault.'[20]

On the other hand, only one of the interviewees used the arguments available in favour of criminalization, particularly invoking the harm principle, to conclude that incest is legitimately criminalized:

> Yes, so far as incest is concerned, there are a number of social harms that are sought to be avoided by prosecuting incest. One is the potential for inbreeding and genetic problems that might result from a pregnancy. The other is the integrity of the family unit and the part that it plays in our kind of society. To prosecute incest reinforces the establishment of the family, the relationships within it, the power relationships that should apply for that unit to operate at its best and to avoid harm to the members of the family unit itself.[21]

Like the original proposal by the MCCOC, all of the other experts who were willing to express a normative position[22] favoured a non-criminal law solution to the

15 See Bronitt and McSherry, above n 1, 602–608; Bernadette McSherry and Bronwyn Naylor, *Australian Criminal Law: Critical Perspectives* (Oxford University Press, Melbourne 2004) 236–238; David Brown et al., *Brown, Farrier, Neal and Weisbrot's Criminal Laws: Materials and Commentary on Criminal Law and Process of New South Wales* (4th edn Federation Press, Leichhardt 2006) 783–784.

16 Bronitt and McSherry, above n 1, 606.

17 McSherry and Naylor, above n 15, 237.

18 Bronitt and McSherry, above n 1, 606; McSherry and Naylor, above n 15, 237.

19 McSherry and Naylor, above n 15, 238; Bronitt and McSherry, above n 1, 606–607.

20 McSherry and Naylor, above n 15, 238.

21 Interview with Nicolas Cowdery (Sydney, 13 August 2007).

22 Two of them did not want to make normative statements on the topic.

problem. It is important to understand however how this argument was formulated. Because there is no generally accepted, established normative concept, arguments against criminalization in this particular case could not be based on such a general theory. Corresponding to the fact that many of the available principles – like the harm principle – can be invoked *in favour* of criminalization, the experts also referred to several different principles when arguing *against* criminal prohibition. Some of them referred to the harm principle, some invoked public interest or offensiveness and others just considered it a moral taboo.

> I do not think incest is legitimately criminalized. I think that is just a moral taboo.[23]

Brent Fisse's statement fits within his general opinion that public morality does not provide a sufficient reason for criminalization in itself.[24] On the other hand, no such normative statements – either on the general principles or on the particular offence of incest – are made in his textbook.[25]

Similar to the discussion of the general limits of criminal law, some of the interviewees presented a mixture of historical explanations for criminalization and a normative position against prohibition:

> In terms of incest, that is a really good example of where it is religious and cultural taboos that have driven criminalization. In modern terms, some of the justifications circulate around genetic risk. That can be addressed in a harm minimization structure through genetic counselling. In some cultures, cousins marry. So it is not a universal norm. And in a multicultural Australia it becomes a question about lower genetic risks in some Australian communities because they are remote and people are marrying distant relatives and so genetic counselling is a general problem not specifically located to just marrying your cousin or having sexual intercourse with your cousin.
>
> The thinking of the Model Criminal Code Officers Committee was to decriminalize it, but, interestingly, out of this very detailed report the only thing that was fixated on in the press was the thought that 'crazy academics were proposing the legalization of incest'. Of course incest is constructed along a range from incest by a father having sexual intercourse with his daughter (which is rape) through to 55-year-old cousins who never met, grew up in different countries, and who meet later in life and fall in love. The failure, in a sense, of the debate to make the disaggregation of these cases led to the withdrawal and revision of that proposal of the report. It is a good example of how sometimes

---

23 Interview with Brent Fisse (Sydney, 22 August 2007).

24 Ibid.

25 Brent Fisse, *Howard's Criminal Law* (5th edn The Law Book Company Limited, Sydney 1990).

> pragmatism prevails, and sometimes moral principle can drive the political process.
>
> The question is, what harm is it causing to others? And it might be that it is creating genetic difficulties. But one of the questions is, how can you minimize that harm? There are technological innovations that can reduce the risk of harm and I think that is the point in the liberal principle always: are there other ways in which harm can be addressed without criminalization and to what extent will criminalization just drive these relationships underground? That produces a whole range of social problems that flow from that, including a proliferation of genetic defects – by criminalizing it, larger problems arise than regulating it (e.g., by requiring genetic counselling before marrying or other things that might be problematic). Also, accepting that there are social and cultural differences around the attitude to marriage between these relatives.
>
> It is not conclusive to say something is harmful to others. You have to ask, what safeguards can be taken apart from the use of criminal law? There is a principle some theorists call the 'principle of parsimony' – to be parsimonious means not to squander. So we should not squander the criminal law. In that sense we should think about ways in which we could achieve the same outcome without criminalization rather than saying: 'yes, I have ticked all the boxes; here is an interest, it is sufficiently harmful, let's criminalize!' Of course the political imperative is always to reassure the community by an act of criminalization. That is an impetus I would like to see diluted in Australia, so that we think twice before criminalization.[26]

After giving historical explanations based on morality, the interviewed academic invoked the harm principle to determine the legitimacy of the offence. Acknowledging that there might be (remote) harm caused by incestuous relationships, he refers to the principle of parsimony in order to limit the scope of the harm principle. Although it is already questionable whether the harm principle itself delivers a legitimate reason for the criminalization of incest, he did not base his critique on a particular definition of 'harm to others', but on the ground that even if there was harm to others the criminal law may not legitimately be used in every case. Again, this normative point of view is not expressed in Australian textbooks.

While this interviewee based his normative critique on a limitation of the harm principle based on the principle of parsimony, David Brown additionally referred to possibilities for diversionary sentencing programs and procedures with respect to incest offences that are already available in practice, and considered the public opinion to be a hindrance for decriminalization. Again, historical explanations for criminalization are given before a normative point of view is presented:

26 Interview with a professor of law at an Australian university (30 August 2007).

> With incest we see the relatively late transference from the ecclesiastical regime through into the criminal law. In England it was not until, I think, 1908, or something like that, that incest was criminalized. Before that it was left to the local priests. And then we see Morris and Hawkins in the 1960s arguing, on their principle, if it is not to do with protection of persons and property, it should be decriminalized. But no politician in their right mind is going to suggest that at the moment. It is interesting to trace that history through.
>
> When we say that it is being criminalized it would be interesting to look at the numbers of prosecutions. Although, yes, it is criminalized, there are a number of process features, like, for example, I think in New South Wales, the Attorney General has to give permission before it can be prosecuted. If it is within the immediate family then offenders are often offered the opportunity to plead guilty and go on a sex offenders program.
>
> Incest is obviously occurring at a much higher rate than ever brought before the notice of the criminal justice system. When it is brought before the criminal justice system it often tends to be diverted in some way, through not being prosecuted or for offenders being channelled into a kind of penal welfare rehabilitative type concern, often in a family setting. So it is not as if it is treated in a really serious way, as a major criminal offence, although it is still on the books.
>
> My personal view would be: incest is clearly an abuse of power. In terms of Morris' and Hawkins' harm principle it is, in most cases, clearly 'harmful', particularly to the younger party involved.
>
> If both parties are adults and the activity is consensual, then there are extra issues about having children and so on. People throw that in as an additional concern. Where there is some form of dysfunctionality that surrounds the particular instance, then, by and large, it is better that that is dealt with in a non-criminal way, through some other form of medical, psychiatric or social-work-type intervention; whatever it might be. Where it is not problematic, where there are no obvious dysfunctional problematic features, then I do not see why it is anyone else's business.[27]

Finally, David Brown referred to the harm principle and concluded that in cases without dysfunctional relations and with genuine consent between adults, there was no reason for criminalization since there was no harm. Interestingly, David Brown did not consider the harm principle to provide the only legitimate reason for criminalization in general, but argued it to be 'very, very difficult to find either any singular principle or, indeed, a set of principles that you can operate in any kind of rationalist way either to explain the content of the existing criminal law as we know it or to guide some ideal criminal law as we might wish it to be'.[28]

27 Interview with David Brown (Sydney, 13 August 2007).

28 Ibid.

On the other hand, he uses the harm principle to criticize the legitimacy of this particular offence. In his textbook such normative statements are also absent.[29]

David Weisbrot also first gave historical explanations for the existence of the taboo. He then referred to the public opinion in favour of criminalization, but finally also invoked the principle of parsimony against prohibition:

> Virtually every human society has some incest taboos and probably those were developed for two reasons. One was a primitive understanding, now a more sophisticated understanding of genetics. And then probably also an understanding on the social side that incest is going to cause social problems, even if you did not understand genetics, much like the adultery example earlier. If you are in a big metropolitan area and there is a falling out, you do not speak to each other anymore – no big deal. If you are in a traditional society where the social networks are critical and where being banned from the society may mean death, then, obviously, those things are much more important. I think that is how it got into the criminal law, apart from the religious understandings.
>
> Now, our understanding of genetics is much more sophisticated and we could probably produce more finely tuned legislation purely from that point of view. I do not think that would change people's minds, particularly that therefore it should be socially acceptable. We have never accepted that it was a defence that you were wearing a condom or you are using birth control or even that it was homosexual intercourse. Those things are still traditional understandings.
>
> With incest, the more distant the relationship is the less any person's concern would be. If you are talking about third cousins twice removed, few people would have any trouble. If you are talking about a close relationship like sister and brother, most people would have an intuitively negative reaction, which is mine. But whether I would want that followed up by a criminal sanction? I think there are many more important things that should be the subject of criminal investigation and punishment.[30]

Dennis Baker took a different approach in order to argue against criminalization. By eliminating questions surrounding harm, he focused on the offensiveness of the behaviour, which he did not consider to provide a legitimate reason for criminalization:

> The example I give to my students is incest between two lesbians. I do that for the simple reason that we do not have to worry about remote harm, for example indirect harm to some offspring that might be born retarded. That way we do not have to worry about harm at all. The only way we look at it is offence. It is offence behind closed doors, in most cases. We might hear about it. We are deeply offended because we find this physically repulsive. There is probably a

29 Brown et al., above n 15.

30 Interview with David Weisbrot (Sydney, 12 September 2007).

> genetic explanation for that. That is not enough to criminalize conduct. You need to show why this conduct is wrongful and there needs to be an objective way to justify invoking the criminal law.
>
> In my opinion, there is no justification for criminalizing incest. As I said earlier, if it was decriminalized it is not going to increase. The numbers will not increase at all. A further problem is enforcement.
>
> … the appropriate response … would be a therapeutic response. I am not saying the state should not be involved, maybe it should be involved. It could be something like a psychiatric, mental health treatment. But there is no role for the criminal law there.[31]

Although this example shows that the harm principle cannot provide a legitimate reason for every case that is punishable as incest, it neglects the question of whether the consideration of harm to others is a legitimate ground for *any* of the cases. In other words, the question of whether possible remote harm that can be caused by acts of incest provides a legitimate reason for criminalization is not answered, but avoided.

Matthew Goode also argued against criminalization by presenting the pragmatic point referred to by the MCCOC as the only possible argument in favour of prohibition:

> No. There is no point. I do not see that it meets any criterion for intervention. The only argument that I ever heard for incest being a criminal offence was a pragmatic one. Very often, not always but very often, adult incest was a product of an unlawful minor incest that they had not caught yet. So it was symptomatic of something that ought to be criminal by the ordinary principles of protecting young people. That was the only argument. I pass on that. I have no practical experience of prosecuting these things. I do not know whether that is true or not, but it is an argument.[32]

Sir Michael Kirby also argued against criminalization for 'real incest cases', referring to merely 'self-regarding' conduct. Finally, his belief that such cases would not be prosecuted in Australia was proved wrong by the recent case discussed above:

> As to incest I think it is generally important to maintain an incest taboo in society. Certainly a lot of the cases we see in the courts nowadays involve offences which are called 'incest'. Typically, they are not truly incest. They are cases of stepfathers or effective stepfathers having sexual intercourse with young girls living with mothers in serial relationships that now exist in our society more frequently than they did in the past. Such offences are very seriously punished

31 Interview with Dennis Baker (Sydney, 20 August 2007).

32 Interview with Matthew Goode (Adelaide, 14 August 2007).

> in Australia. That punishment is usually justified by the need to protect young and vulnerable children, particularly from offenders in positions of trust. So far as that object of the law is concerned that is certainly an other-regarding activity. Therefore I am in favour of the availability of the criminal law in such cases. However, if it got to the point that the person was 18 years or more, then the mere fact that there was an 'incest' act would not, in my opinion, attract justifiable criminal punishment. If people are adults, or of full age of consent and understanding and have a sexual relationship by consent with each other in private, I do not think, in the words of the Wolfenden report, that it is the law's business to intrude into such cases. I believe that, in Australia, generally, such conduct would not be the subject of a criminal prosecution even if, within the words of a statute, an offence exists. I do not think that the accused would be prosecuted if the persons were adults of full understanding and capacity and were consenting to private sexual activity. Nevertheless, clearly the law has a purpose to protect the under-aged. Therefore, whether it is in a true 'incest' situation or a fictional incest situation of serial relationships and a person involved is underage, that needs protection.[33]

Also against criminalization on a normative level, but invoking the public opinion as a hindrance for decriminalization, was Ian Leader-Elliott:

> I do not think incest should be criminalized. There is, of course, a serious problem about protecting individuals from misuse of familial power, influence or authority. I am quite unsure about the age of consent and equally unsure about the relevance of age differences or generational differences. It is the business of law reformers to work out solutions to these problems. That would be a prerequisite for legalization. If I think about the prospects for legalization, I am uncertain, however, whether it would be possible to work out solutions to those issues unless there was, in the first place, a culture of acceptance for incest and incestuous relationships. It may be that it is simply not possible to devise rules for informed consent unless we have existing models of acceptable practice. We could try to extrapolate from non-incestuous relationships – but that may simply not work. That is to say – maybe social acceptance has to precede legalization.
>
> Interestingly, the Model Criminal Code Officers Committee made a recommendation to eliminate the offence, when consenting adults were involved. So also, I think, the Royal Commission on Human Relationships, back in the late 1970s. The public reaction to those proposals was remarkable for its ferocity.[34]

Taking into consideration that most of the interviewees argued against criminalization, but were referring to several different principles and arguments, two conclusions can be drawn. First of all, the predominance of historical

33 Interview with Sir Michael Kirby (Sydney, 24 July 2007).

34 Interview with Ian Leader-Elliott (Adelaide, 14 August 2007).

explanations for criminalization apparent in the Australian literature is also reflected by many of the responses given by the interviewees. Asked about the legitimacy of the offence, several of the interviewees started their statements with a description of historical reasons for criminalization. Like the discussion on the general limits in the textbooks, the available principles were used to *describe* why conduct was made criminal.

But in contrast to the textbook presentation of the general principles, finally, the majority of the interviewees also articulated a normative point of view and argued against the criminalization of sexual conduct between consenting adult relatives. The obvious problem in making such an argument, though, is that the principles that can be invoked in favour of criminalization are not generally considered to be illegitimate reasons for prohibition of any conduct. As such, the view in favour of decriminalization cannot be articulated in a stringent normative argumentation, so long as the principles invoked are not questioned with respect to their general normative legitimacy, but only used in a descriptive way. In other words, while, for example, Nicholas Cowdery invoked the harm principle in favour of criminalization, others, like David Brown and Sir Michael Kirby, particularly referred to the harm principle when arguing against criminalization. But none of them based their opinion on a generally formulated concept of the harm principle. In contrast, David Brown and another interviewed professor of law at an Australian university particularly argued that the harm principle was not the only reason for legitimate criminalization. Others, like Brent Fisse and Dennis Baker, referred to public morality (or offensiveness) to conclude that the offence was illegitimate. But none of the Australian texts argues that either public morality or offensiveness do not provide a good reason for criminalization. Finally, when the public interest was invoked as an explanation for criminalization in practice, the pragmatic reason discussed in Chapter 4 is presented as a hindrance for normative theorizing again.

Besides the focus on influences on the legislative practice, the obvious problem is that, even among the supporters of a non-criminal law solution, there is no agreement on why, in general, certain kinds of conduct should (or should not) be criminalized.

Because all of the principles themselves are used to *describe* reasons for criminalization and not to make normative statements on its legitimacy, none of them is regarded to be illegitimate in general, but all of them can be invoked to legitimate individual crimes too. Particularly with incest, this leads to the paradoxical situation that, despite the general opinion among the interviewees being against criminalization, the textbooks, when dealing with normative statements at all, describe the arguments to be 'finely balanced' and it is even argued that a 'practical advantage' in relation to the difficulties in proving non-consent would tip the scales in favour of criminalization of a consensual behaviour. Despite the majority of the interviewees being against criminalization of incest, the lack of a general normative concept also leads to the lack of normative critique articulated in the textbooks in this particular case.

Bestiality

Sexual intercourse with animals remains a criminal offence in Australia, while it was decriminalized in Germany in 1969. The reason for its abolition in Germany was the acknowledgment that the prohibition was based only on public morality.[35] This is further illustrated by the fact that cruelty to animals remains a criminal offence – no matter if it is caused by sexual or non-sexual behaviour.[36]

The offence of bestiality is not discussed in the standard Australian criminal law texts. The interviews revealed that while the supporters of criminalization mainly refer to the cruelty aspect, the opponents claim (in conformity with the German approach) that the offence is based only on public morality and that the cruelty aspect only provides for the criminalization of any act of cruelty to animals but not any act of bestiality:

> As far as bestiality is concerned, I think that is easier. I myself whilst finding it personally repulsive, would not criminalize it, because, if bestiality is to be dealt with it should be dealt with under cruelty to animals type legislation. I am a patron of the RSPCA Australia so I am not in favour of cruelty to animals, including sexual cruelty. Animals are sentient beings. They are deserving of our respect. But it is not enough in my judgement that, because I get upset or find things repulsive, that one should criminalize it. Therefore I would not do so in that case.[37]
>
> I have not really had occasion to think much about bestiality, but that would be problematic, too, unless there is some secular form of harm to the animal.[38]
>
> Concerning bestiality, I have never heard an argument for criminalizing it at all. … I suppose it is against public moral values. But what else is against public moral values? Public moral values count a great deal because scandal drives change. If there is a big enough uproar then governments have to do something, particularly populist ones. The pressure is driven by the media, by talk-back radio and all that sort of thing. So public moral values count, but I have not heard anyone getting upset about this for quite a while – maybe for 40 years. On the other hand, they get upset about home invasions, vandalizing motorcars and

---

35 See Claus Roxin, *Strafrecht, Allgemeiner Teil, Band I: Grundlagen, Aufbau der Verbrechenslehre* (4th edn C.H. Beck, Munich 2006) 19–20.

36 § 17 *Tierschutzgesetz* (Protection of Animals Act):
'Whoever
1. kills a vertebrate without reasonable cause or
2. causes a vertebrate
   (a) significant pain or suffering out of brutality or
   (b) prolonged or repetitive significant pain or suffering

shall be punished with imprisonment of not more than three years or a fine.'

37 Interview with Sir Michael Kirby (Sydney, 24 July 2007).

38 Interview with Brent Fisse (Sydney, 22 August 2007).

> all sorts of other things, which are perfectly sensible things to get upset about. 'Public moral values' is too broad a category.[39]

In contrast to this view and indeed supporting prohibition, Ian Leader-Elliott argued that cruelty to animals alone actually legitimates the offence of bestiality:

> Bestiality has always troubled me. We are talking about private bestiality – there's no question of causing offence by a public spectacle. We do not have a consenting subject here. We cannot conceive of an animal deriving any pleasure from this. The animal probably would be terrified and suffer injury. There are very serious issues of cruelty here that might tend to be neglected because people think of this as primarily an offence of sexual immorality.
>
> I think bestiality should be a criminal offence. That is on the ground of cruelty. I cannot think of any reservations or qualifications that could take it out of the area of cruelty. We may reach a stage, in the not too distant future, where the laws against bestiality will have to be sustained on the ground that cruelty cannot be justified. Cruelty aside, the moral arguments against bestiality seem inherently unstable. It takes very little imagination indeed to contemplate the possibility that bestiality might figure in a rock concert, a circus performance or as a variety of performance art. Entertainment always pushes at moral limits and delights in giving offence. But cruelty is something else again.[40]

Even if it were correct that one 'cannot think of any reservations or qualifications that could take it out of the area of cruelty', the question of why an offence of bestiality is necessary remains. If every act of bestiality was also an act of cruelty to animals, a general offence of cruelty to animals would cover all the acts of bestiality as well.

Similarly neglecting this point and additionally referring to the welfare principle, another academic also argued in favour of criminalization:

> Bestiality is a good example. Welfare – it depends how you define welfare – but the welfare to the animal is an issue. I just think it is extraordinarily cruel. Concepts of consent can really only be understood in human terms, I think. And the dignity of the animal is an important factor. I see it in those terms.[41]

Although not considering the problems surrounding the cruelty argument, Dennis Baker argued in favour of a non-criminal law solution, focusing on the treatment of the psychological problems that are causing such behaviour:

---

39 Interview with Matthew Goode (Adelaide, 14 August 2007).

40 Interview with Ian Leader-Elliott (Adelaide, 14 August 2007).

41 Interview with a professor of law at an Australian university (30 August 2007).

> Bestiality is slightly different. We might say the animal has been harmed. We have seen, in England, fox hunting has been criminalized. Bull fighting is a sport in Spain that some say should be criminalized. It is not use of an animal for a real purpose. I think we might have a duty not to harm animals. But I have not got right into that.
>
> But even if we say that this is harm to animals, the appropriate response, again, would be some psychiatric order. Not many people engage in this conduct and it is usually stimulated by some sort of psychological problem and therefore – and that might seem narrow, but it is a basic fact that people are not attracted to animals unless they have got some sort of mental problem – let the courts make some sort of civil order to compel the individual to seek psychiatric treatment if the problem is serious enough.[42]

While Ian Leader-Elliott based his opinion in favour of criminalization solely on the cruelty aspect and rejected moral arguments as a legitimate reason, Nicholas Cowdery considers both to provide good reasons for prohibition:

> Bestiality. Fortunately we do not see much of it in this community. At least not much comes to prosecution. I guess for a number of practical and moral reasons, bestiality is objectionable. Somebody might ask: what is the harm in that conduct? I have not thought about it until now. I suppose it arises from the fact that humans regard themselves as being at the top of the evolutionary tree with the duty to other species to protect them and not abuse them and not subject them to unreasonable or improper conduct, pain and suffering. I guess it is really the protection of other species from harm that is in the centre of making that conduct criminal. In addition, you have the moral and the ethical arguments as well, and the standard setting of the criminal law in the community generally. But, I have been here nearly 13 years and I have only had two or three cases of bestiality from around the state.[43]

David Brown refers to the symbolical use of the criminal law in this area before arguing against criminalization:

> Bestiality is interesting, too. Clearly, historically, it was massively committed, particularly in peasant society, and still is in those countries with large rural populations that do still have designated occupational positions like goat herders and so on. It is clearly a widespread activity and very few people are ever brought before the criminal law. Therefore, you have to wonder what it is about those particular cases. Often there is a whole range of other things going on, local things that are being fought out. Whenever you are in that situation where you have got a significantly occurring activity, but only a very, very small proportion

42 Interview with Dennis Baker (Sydney, 20 August 2007).

43 Interview with Nicolas Cowdery (Sydney, 13 August 2007).

> of prosecutions, then you have got all the conditions for the symbolic use of the criminal law, for stigmatizing particular people, for acting out reprisals and vendettas and so on. That has got very little to do with the actual nature of the behaviour.
>
> Having said all that, of course, it is becoming questioned for a whole lot of other reasons: the increasing concern about animals as a sort of 'subject'. Not really yet as legal subjects, although we just had a conference here on 'animals as legal subjects'. There is an increasing concern about cruelty to animals – how they are kept and how they are killed for the market and so on. It runs alongside the whole emergence of the human rights debate, I suppose. The discussion on animal rights is, to an extent, broadly progressive. In that context we may be more likely to see greater enforcement of that legislation. The only case I can think of, recently in New South Wales, was the guy with the rabbits. He actually ended up being acquitted on the ground of mental illness. Clearly, he would have had a very, very hard time in jail, if he had been sent to prison. It is maybe better to deal with this kind of 'disturbance' in a context of medical treatment, which is, of course, what eventually happens.
>
> Should the criminal law be used? Again, I would say, historically, by and large, it has not. The criminal law sanction against bestiality has been largely symbolic. Where it has not been symbolic it has been discriminatory and punitive and the vehicle for settling a whole lot of other scores that had nothing much to do with the actual offence. Ultimately, I think, this is something that should be better dealt with through other forms of regulation, like codes of practice and so on. And where particular instances of repeated and exploited damaging behaviour come to light, I would look for some social or medical intervention rather than the criminal law. I cannot see how the criminal law is really of much assistance in this area.[44]

Unfortunately, David Brown did not base his objection to the offence on a normative concept. By stating that he 'cannot see how the criminal law is really of much assistance in this area' the question arises, assistance in achieving what, the enforcement of public moral values or the prevention of harm to animals? In other words, what is the general purpose of the criminal law or the particular purpose of this prohibition, which Brown does not see served by the offence?

Finally, David Weisbrot, without making a normative statement on the legitimacy of the offence, once again, invoked the public opinion as an obstacle for decriminalization in practice:

> It is often used as a joke in Western societies. Australians love to make jokes about New Zealanders and sheep. And there is only the rare, rare case you see reported. There was actually one not so long ago in Australia. A stockbroker who

44 Interview with David Brown (Sydney, 13 August 2007).

> was an ice addict was buying rabbits and sexually mutilating them. Obviously a very disturbed individual.
>
> But do we keep those on the criminal side of the ledger? Again, I suspect you would have difficulty moving them off. Largely because people would say, even if there is only a case once a decade, nevertheless as a society we are making certain statements by prohibiting these kinds of behaviours. So I suspect it would be very hard to get a Western government to actually take the step of decriminalizing this. And being a politician, why would you? It is not exactly one of the great social movements.
>
> I find it hard to take it too seriously as a matter that the police should be investigating and prosecuting. But if given to me to recommend to the Government, recognizing popular opinion and culture and so on, I think it would be very, very hard to recommend decriminalization of either incest or bestiality.[45]

Similar to incest, the vast majority of the interviewees argued against the criminalization of bestiality. A further similarity was that different principles (particularly the harm principle and public morality) were considered to provide arguments in favour of criminalization. Finally, the political reality and the public interest were invoked again.

The reason bestiality was chosen as an example here is that its legitimacy is discussed by invoking similar arguments as made with respect to incest. But one major difference from incest is that bestiality was decriminalized in Germany in 1969. Because bestiality was decriminalized in Germany, while cruelty to animals remains a criminal offence, the two main arguments brought up in favour of criminalization do not pass a reality test. First, the prevention of cruelty to animals is no reason to have a bestiality offence. Not every sexual practice inflicts pain and not every act of cruelty to animals is sexual. Therefore, cruelty to animals can be dealt with comprehensively without the existence of a bestiality offence. Secondly, the often stated argument that one would probably not see bestiality decriminalized because of political reality is proved false by the German criminal law reform in 1969.

The only plausible way to normatively legitimate the offence of bestiality seems to be the acknowledgement of public morality as a reason for criminalization. But, except for Nicholas Cowdery, all the interviewees who made a normative statement[46] refused to legitimate the offence by reference to public morality – even when arguing in favour of criminalization. Once again, the rejection of public morality as a legitimate ground for a criminal offence articulated in the interviews is not represented in the Australian textbooks where the principle is mainly used as a descriptive tool.

---

45 Interview with David Weisbrot (Sydney, 12 September 2007).

46 Nine out of eleven did.

Possession of Illicit Drugs

> My answer is, I do not have a strong personal view. I have never needed to develop a strong personal view. If I was the dictator of this country I would think long and hard about the various factors that I have been discussing and I would want expert assistance on the availability of other alternatives and the likely pragmatic consequences of adopting different strategies designed to achieve the ultimate goal, which would be to discourage or reduce consumption of dangerous drugs.[47]

The possession of illicit drugs for the purpose of self-administration is criminal both in Australia and Germany. In Germany, within the framework of the *Rechtsgutstheorie*, attempts were made to justify the offence by establishing the health of the nation or a drug-free society as a legitimate legal good/interest. Criticism of the creation of an abstract *Kollektivrechtsgut* as an illegitimate attempt to avoid problems surrounding the criminalization of consensual self-harm was discussed above.

In Australia, the concept of harm minimization is very influential. 'Harm minimisation balances the harms of drug use against the harms caused by prohibition.'[48] But the concept, which has influenced the Australian drug laws and political discussion on the issue, is also criticized. It is argued that 'weighing and aggregating different types of harm is an impossible task'.[49]

However, the responses given by the experts when asked about the legitimacy of the prohibition against possession of drugs demonstrated the problems caused by the lack of a normative concept in the Australian approach to identifying limits of criminal law. The best example for this is provided by the answer of a professor of law at an Australian university. After identifying several possible reasons for criminalization, and even after expressing a personal view, the second step required to make a normative statement, the normative assessment of the available reasons, is not taken:

> It is framed always in abstract terms about harm and what harms flow from, like loss of productivity, mental dysfunction or disease or mental illness. There is a whole range of contested and unexplored things. It is difficult to say whether the people who take drugs were like that before. There is not necessarily a good control group when you look at the drug-using community. And there is the association with crime, the crime-drug-nexus and so on. But, of course, you do not know. A drug life tends to be sustained by a life of crime. People do justify it in those terms, but in the end I do not see that as terribly compelling. I think that it tends to be now justified in moral terms because people have reached

47 Interview with Stephen Odgers (Sydney, 27 August 2007).

48 Bronitt and McSherry, above n 1, 787.

49 Ibid.

> the point, pretty much, where the ingestion of tobacco is almost becoming a moral wrong. In relation to certain categories of drugs it is a moral wrong. That is hardly contestable as a proposition, but that is how people – if you did an empirical study of attitudes to drug use, I would guarantee the overwhelming majority of people would say that drug use is morally wrong, irrespective of whether it is causing harm others or harm to the individual.
>
> So does that justify it? Personally, the principle of pragmatism would be my favourite one and I would want to seek to regulate it. The pleasure aspects of drugs are inherent, universal across cultures. I would rather regulate than proscribe because of the unintended effects of proscription. But either of those principles *could* justify it. All the arguments given are refutable, but you certainly *could* justify it in those terms.[50]

Within the last paragraph of the quote, the crucial difference between the German and the Australian perspective becomes obvious: while Australian scholars, independent of their personal opinion, present different principles that are all considered to be able to justify an offence, their German colleagues will make normative statements to argue for their opinion and against the opposing views.

Without making a normative statement, but only describing the motives for criminalization, Sir Gerard Brennan combined paternalistic arguments with the welfare principle:

> Again, I would like to have a look at the history – but the history is all fairly recent on this one. I would suspect that the justification is that by proscribing that conduct there is an inhibition on the ingestion of drugs, which, if not controlled, would impose, not only on the individual but on the community, an intolerable burden. On the individual in terms of their mental and physical conditions and on the community in terms of the care that has to then be given to those who are affected.[51]

As discussed above, the main concern of the *Rechtsgutstheorie* regarding this offence is the fact that deliberate self-harm is not considered to justify criminalization and, according to that, paternalism is generally rejected as a reason for prohibiting conduct.

This view is also shared by Nicholas Cowdery, Brent Fisse and, particularly, Dennis Baker:

> I do not think anything can justify the criminalization of the self-administration of illicit drugs. I think the self-administrators are doing all the harm to themselves. It is not being done by somebody else. I think it is quite inappropriate to

50 Interview with a professor of law at an Australian university (30 August 2007).

51 Interview with Sir Gerard Brennan (Sydney, 15 August 2007).

> criminalize it. It should be dealt with as a medical and social issue, quite apart from the criminal law, in my view.
>
> I take a different attitude to the supply for profit of drugs. I think that should be criminalized because of the harm caused to others. But possession of quantities for self-administration, I do not think should be criminalized.[52]

> I think that it is difficult again when you have got people consenting, if it is an informed consent. If it is not informed consent, non-criminal means of social control could and should be used. But if it is consensual, I do not see any rational distinction between that sort of behaviour and many other behaviours that are not criminalized, like people flying light aeroplanes, mountain climbing, swimming on dangerous beaches and so on. The fact that you get more people who harm themselves consensually through drugs, I do not think that really affects the argument. Taking alcohol is, I suppose, the most obvious.
>
> That is not to say that there should not be a lot of civil means of assisting people and trying to prevent that sort of behaviour.[53]

> There is no principle to justify the criminalization of self-harm. The basic reason for this is (Feinberg wrote a whole volume on this and I agree with him although I critique his other volumes): you have already harmed yourself so sending someone to jail is another great harm. Do two wrongs make a right? They do not. The person is already a vulnerable person who may have attempted suicide, may have a disorder where they are cutting their arms and so on. They need help. They do not need further harm. But that is what sending someone to jail and giving them a criminal record is: it is harming them. It has severe consequences. Criminal records mean you cannot travel to America. If you are an Australian citizen with a criminal record, America will not take you. So your liberty is restricted for the rest of your life. Your chances of seeking employment are reduced. You are stigmatized. And that does not even include the very rough time you can have in jail. Therefore, there is no moral justification for inflicting further harm on someone who has harmed themselves. They are not harming anyone else. I do not think there is anything that can justify this.[54]

A slightly different perspective was presented by David Brown, Ian Leader-Elliott and David Weisbrot. Although they also opposed a criminal offence, they all referred to different definitions of the term harm to others, which could be used to include indirect harms, such as harms to society due to the consumption of drugs:

52 Interview with Nicolas Cowdery (Sydney, 13 August 2007).
53 Interview with Brent Fisse (Sydney, 22 August 2007).
54 Interview with Dennis Baker (Sydney, 20 August 2007).

One used to say, under Mill's version of the harm principle, which ran contrary to criminalization, the idea that people could go to hell in their own way.

Now, of course, everyone is more concerned about it. Legitimately, I think, we can draw 'harm' in more nebulous ways like, at a crude level, I suppose, economic harms, the cost of hospital treatment, the loss of the person's capacity to be productive, the capacity to live a full and interesting and useful life and so on. Now, the boundaries of the harm principle have been pushed out to encompass those sorts of 'harms'. And once you do that, then, I guess, on that reasoning it is legitimate for the state to make a stand. Again, that is where I would be more inclined to fall back on these more pragmatic, what I would call 'process concerns'; like the second one: 'is the mischief better dealt with under existing legislation or by using other remedies.'

For personal use, not that you want to medicalize everything, but it seems better to conceive individual drug use as predominately a cultural phenomenon about means of pleasure and how you cope with life. It is increasingly a matter of a kind of consumer choice about how you construct pleasure. I do not see that the criminal law assists very much to have this behaviour criminalized on an individual level. I can see the point of having sanctions which may be, at least partly, criminal at the level of importation and distribution of drugs. When it comes down to the individual, there are maybe instances where it is useful because it acts as a point of intervention, which then leads to someone getting into a drug rehab program or whatever.

By and large it seems that the criminal law is not being of great assistance in a more rational sort of approach to the problem, which tries to minimize harm as the major concern.[55]

In general, my attitude is that self-administration of drugs should not be a criminal offence. Of course, everyone in Australia must be troubled by self-administration of alcohol by Aboriginal people. The temptation to move in and say no – consumption is an offence – is very strong indeed. But my bias is probably still the same – that other methods should be tried rather than prohibitions against use. Alcohol in the Aboriginal community is no different from heroin or cocaine in this community.

I think the self-administration of drugs should not be criminalized, but how you actually solve the practical problems is another question. Our preferred approach is to distinguish between the illicit supplier and the user and penalize the supplier. The social costs associated with anti-trafficking laws are huge and well known. But there seems no alternative – those costs have to be borne in order to maintain limits on harmful consumption.[56]

55 Interview with David Brown (Sydney, 13 August 2007).
56 Interview with Ian Leader-Elliott (Adelaide, 14 August 2007).

> On a pure libertarian model or harm model, if you are saying that the persons are only hurting themselves it is difficult to justify. I think nowadays people would seek external justifications. There is also social harm that is caused because of the person withdrawing from useful labour, the effects on family, the effects on the health system and so on. I think those arguments can be made. I think you have to look at the individual cases. Where people are using drugs that really do produce a significant possibility of criminal activity or harm to others (like ice) then you are more likely to be interventionist. If someone is using analgesics without a script for pain relief, then it becomes harder to argue that that is a true 'criminal matter'.[57]

An additional point was raised by Matthew Goode who, opposing the offence in general, presented an idea that could justify criminalization detached from any of the discussed principles – 'flouting of the law':

> I have no idea. The only way I could think of that might possibly be is that it flouts the law. If you decide that cannabis is sufficiently nasty that you are going to prohibit trading and possession and all the rest of it – outlaw it – if you decide that, assuming that, then the sight of someone puffing away on a cannabis cigarette in the middle of town offends. Not because it is offensive in the sense that bestiality might be – shocking; but because it cannot be tolerated because what it does is it flouts that original decision. And that is behind attempts to ban cannabis and cocaine implements, which is currently taking place across the country. There are places which sell 'cocaine kits', which are nothing more or less than a bit of glass, a razorblade and a straw. They sell all these things, which are perfectly innocuous and you can make them up yourself. Why would you criminalize that? Because it is an insult and it says: 'bugger you!'[58]

Finally, a practice-based answer was given by Sir Michael Kirby:

> In most of the cases, at least in those that come before the courts, the situation is not easy because the factual evidence tends to indicate that the persons involved are not only securing drugs for their own use, but are trading in drugs, sometimes to fund their own drug use. Therefore, if you adopt an 'other-regarding' test and even one of proportionality, there is no doubt that there is usually an effect on other people; if only in sustaining a market in such drugs.
>
> The benign approach to drugs such as cannabis has run into a problem because we now know that long-term cannabis use has, in certain people who are vulnerable to this, serious implications for schizophrenia and other medical conditions. So, prohibited drugs, hallucinatory and other drugs, are generally not good for people.

57 Interview with David Weisbrot (Sydney, 12 September 2007).

58 Interview with Matthew Goode (Adelaide, 14 August 2007).

Now, there are, of course, a lot of things that are not good for you. You could probably construct a good argument that driving a car is not good for you. Lots of people die as a result of it. But we do not criminalize that activity. So it is just a question of deciding upon prohibitions in each case. I have sometimes asked myself why it was, when I was a member of the Council of Civil Liberties in the 1960s, nobody talked about homosexual offences. What are the things that we do not talk about now, that we do not see now, but which our successors will talk about in 40 years time and then look back and wonder why we did not see with sharp clarity the unfairness and wrongness of our approaches? It has sometimes occurred to me, for example, that our approach to drug use as a criminal law issue (as distinct from as a public health issue) may, in years to come, be seen as just such an instance. That possibility therefore leads on to the prospect that drugs constitute one issue we will need to reconsider.

After all, the prohibitionist model effectively began in the State of Maine in the United States in the 1830s. It then eventually spread to other states of the United States and ultimately to their great national experiment with Prohibition which was then abandoned. This was the progenitor for the international approach, strongly supported by the United States of America in international agencies of the United Nations and in treaties, for a prohibitionist model binding on the whole world. What they abandoned in their own country is now their gift to the rest of the world. The United States insist upon it and so do many other countries, including my own. There is, no doubt, a very great need to deal with the issues of the use of prohibited drugs and dependence by young and vulnerable people. If you love them you will seek to protect them. However, the question still remaining is: is the criminal law the right methodology? Is it pussyfooting and weak to say that we should only use public health measures? Do you have to take these strong measures of the criminal law because of the large markets that exist? Do those large markets exist because there are very many decent citizens who are using these drugs, which obviously give them some pleasure and satisfaction? Is it the law's business to stop them from using them, if they can perform their ordinary lives as citizens with the use of these drugs? These are very complicated issues.

There have been major inquiries in Canada and elsewhere, including in Australia, on these subjects. It is simply a matter of trying to work out where the balance of harm lies and whether our current strategies are justifiable, effective and proportionate. There are arguments that we do not have a correct balance. However, the law is as it is. Of course my duty as a judge is to obey the law and to apply it. This I do, but generally with a lighter touch than some judges who apply drug laws with great enthusiasm. I do so without enthusiasm; but because it is the law.[59]

59 Interview with Sir Michael Kirby (Sydney, 24 July 2007).

Similar to their view on the offences of incest and bestiality, the vast majority of the interviewees were against criminalization of possession of illicit drugs. While some of them only referred to paternalism as not providing a legitimate reason for prohibition, others also considered in their statements possible remote harms to others.

Opinions Without Conceptual Theory

The general difference between the jurisprudential, normative approach taken by the *Rechtsgutstheorie* and the criminological, descriptive one used in Australia becomes sizeable when looking at particular offences.

Again, it becomes obvious that it is not the differences of opinion regarding the content of the limits of criminal law that are crucial. Instead, it is the methods applied that are fundamentally different. Despite the lack of a general normative concept, critical opinions on the legitimate scope of the criminal law are also present among Australian lawyers.

All three offences discussed in this chapter are subject to criticism in both Australia and Germany. But while the *Rechtsgutstheorie* provides German lawyers with an acknowledged method of articulating their arguments, Australians face severe difficulties in making a normative point because the scope of accepted arguments is not limited on a general level, and every possible descriptive principle can be invoked as a reason for criminalization. In this way, some interviewees referred to several different principles in order to make the same argument and some referred to the same principle in order to conclude the opposite. The only communality between the forms of argumentation is the fact that none of the experts expounded a normative concept on which to base their critique. All of them simply referred to a suitable principle without generally defining its terms. The best example for this is the harm principle: none of the interviewees presented an elaborated concept of the principle in order to make their argument. In contrast, all of them confirmed their own concerns. As seen in Chapter 4, when experts were asked about the general legitimacy of the principle, a common answer referred to the problems surrounding the definition of the term harm to others and the uncertain scope of the principle that flows from that. Now, when discussing the legitimacy of particular offences, these exact concerns were seen in practice: the harm principle was invoked for and against criminalization because no concept, no definition of the term harm to others was applied, but only a 'nebulous'[60] notion of harm was referred to for different purposes.

In accordance with this lack of a general concept, and despite an apparent rejection of the offences among the interviewees, the criminal law texts – the main source from which students (future lawyers) receive their information – do not make normative statements in favour of or against criminalization, but (if they

60 Interview with David Brown (Sydney, 13 August 2007).

discuss it at all) only describe the historical reasons for a prohibition. Based on this, law students are not encouraged to take a normative point of view themselves, but only to know possible reasons in favour of criminalization. Thus, lawyers are not taught to question the law as it stands, but only to be able to describe its development as a political exercise.

The prime example of this attitude was given by Stephen Odgers:

> You are asking me a philosophical question concerning legal theory. I have very little expertise in that area and indeed I approach it with a degree of cynicism. As a practical lawyer I deal with the laws as they stand and as I am forced to when representing clients and acting on their behalf. We can engage in lots of intellectual debate about what the criminal law should be, but, as I have explained, at the end of the day, it is a political question. And absent constitutional constraints, if the Parliament wants to criminalize conduct it can! End of story.[61]

61 Interview with Stephen Odgers (Sydney, 27 August 2007).

Chapter 6
Conclusions

> First, it is critical in legal studies not to surrender leadership to the courts and legislatures. The academic branch of the profession has an independent responsibility to think and write creatively about the law without simply copying sources used by lawyers. This is a hard lesson to learn in the English-speaking world, but it is taken for granted on the Continent.[1]

Summary – The Lack of a Normative Concept

> It appears that Australian criminal law scholars consider their task to consist solely of the application and interpretation of valid law, and that they leave criminal legal policy entirely to the legislature. My position, as is known, is different. Perhaps through your experiences in Australia it will become clear to you why German criminal law scholarship has resonated influentially in many countries while Australian criminal law scholarship is unknown outside Australia.[2]

During the analysis it became clear that normative statements on the legitimate limits of criminal law are not part of legal culture and education in Australia. While the historical neglect of questions concerning legal theory in general has been overcome in recent years, today the issue is approached in a descriptive, explanatory way, using criminology as the wider framework for the discussion.

As the examples of incest, bestiality and possession of drugs have shown, the lack of articulated normative concepts is not due to the absence of opinion on the issue. Instead, it is based on the predominance of criminological approaches rather than the jurisprudential emphasis present in the German discussion. This also leads to the fact that Australian criminal lawyers – particularly practitioners, but also academics – do not consider it to be their function to make normative statements on the limits of criminal law.

---

1 George P. Fletcher, *The Grammar of Criminal Law: American, Comparative and International* (Oxford University Press, Oxford, New York 2007) xiv.

2 Statement by Claus Roxin (personal email correspondence, 8 June 2007): 'Es verhält sich wohl so, dass die australischen Strafrechtler ihre Aufgabe nur in der Anwendung und Auslegung des geltenden Rechts sehen und die Kriminalpolitik ganz dem Gesetzgeber überlassen. Mein Standpunkt ist das bekanntlich nicht. Vielleicht wird Ihnen aus Ihren australischen Erfahrungen auch erklärlich, warum die deutsche Strafrechtswissenschaft in vielen Ländern so große Resonanz findet, die australische aber außerhalb Australiens unbekannt ist.'

The purpose of this analysis is neither to identify one of the investigated approaches as being 'right' nor to say that only one of them leads to 'correct' results. Instead, it has to be emphasized that both approaches have advantages and disadvantages. While in Germany criminological aspects are largely underrepresented, in Australia jurisprudential elements are lacking.

In Australia, possible reasons for the criminalization of certain conduct are *described*, while no normative statements on the legitimacy of the reasons are made. This provides for a comprehensive analysis of the history and the politics of criminal law.

In Germany, legitimate reasons for criminalization of conduct are established in order to make statements on the legitimacy of particular offences. This provides a framework for legislative critique.

While the Australian approach aims to *describe* the politics of criminalization, the German one aims to *influence* these politics. Which particular version of the *Rechtsgut* concept provides the 'correct' answer to all questions on the legitimacy of criminal offences was not the topic of this analysis. In contrast, the ongoing and, in recent times, even increased debate among German criminal lawyers about the definition of the term *Rechtsgut* and its capability to adapt to developments in modern science and society indicates that currently there is no version of the concept on which a general consensus might be obtained. However, the debate itself is part of the legal culture in Germany and it embodies the understanding that the question of legitimate limits of the criminal law is a component of legal science, education and practice. This is the crucial difference to the situation in Australia where no such normative debate is being conducted.

Outlook – A Unique Opportunity

This book started as a project that aimed to enhance the German *Rechtsgutstheorie* by analysing the Australian perspective on the limits of criminal law. It ended as a critique of the descriptive approach taken in Australia. The critique does not concern the contents of the discussion, it concerns the anti-normative methodology used. The ideas are present, and the forums exist as well. What is missing is someone to start a normative discussion on general limits of criminal law.

In fact, Australia currently has a significant advantage with regard to the development of criminal law theory. First of all, the lack of an established concept provides an opportunity for an 'unpolluted' start to the discussion. Problems that the *Rechtsgutstheorie* faces because of its long tradition stemming from the Enlightenment can be avoided when developing a new, contemporary concept that considers issues surrounding modern developments, technologies, etc. right from the beginning.

Secondly, the trend towards codification of criminal law in Australia provides a practical opportunity for legal theory. Of the nine Australian jurisdictions, three still do not have a criminal code. Without knowing whether these states will eventually introduce a criminal code or whether legislating criminal law might one day even become a federal power so that only one criminal code would apply across Australia, the lack of codification in all jurisdictions poses a practical challenge for a legal theory dealing with the limits of criminal law. Therefore, criminal law theory actually might have a higher chance of influencing practice. This might be particularly attractive to Australian scholars who often emphasize pragmatic reasons for their neglect of the topic. It is also important to emphasize, again, that invoking the lack of a Bill of Rights in Australia as an obstacle to legal theorizing on the legitimate limits of the criminal law is counterproductive. Of course, if there were a Bill of Rights such theorizing would have a suitable starting point and it would be easier to produce legal arguments. However, as normative criminal law theory is independent of the existence of a Bill of Rights, such theorizing can actually support the pursuit of enacting one. Normative theories, based for example, on social contract theory, can establish certain criteria to identify illegitimate acts of criminalization. If such findings cannot invoke existing constitutional rights for their support, they actually may provide further reasons to introduce a Bill of Rights. Once again, influencing legislation and decision-making by the courts is not a requirement, but a goal of normative legal theorizing.

Of course, when one considers the extent of their influence on the decisions of the courts, the role of legal scholars is different in Germany compared to that of their counterparts in Anglophone countries. German courts, for example, routinely cite academic works in their judgements – sometimes in support of their rulings, sometimes as references for dissenting opinions. In English-speaking countries, on the other hand, the courts generally only refer to other judgements to support their rulings. While, from a continental lawyer's perspective, such neglect of the work by experts in the field who have devoted their careers to the development of just solutions for legal problems seems to amount to a squandering of resources, it is not the intention of this analysis to attempt to change this historically grown understanding. However, by invoking the courts' independence of academic opinion as a reason for their refusal to engage in normative discussions on legitimate limits of the criminal law, Australian lawyers seem to underestimate the influence which they already have. Every judge and every law reformer, as well as many members of parliament who actually participate in the process of law-making, have studied law at university. What they have learned there will inevitably influence their (future) decisions. Therefore, even without being explicitly acknowledged in court rulings, academics already do influence the development of the criminal law in English-speaking countries, too.

The *Rechtsgutstheorie*'s advantage is its structure. It provides a basis for reasoned discussion and a method of legal argumentation to identify, analyse and critique legislative decisions. It certainly does not provide the perfect answer to every question concerning criminal law policy and its critics invoke considerable arguments. But the *Rechtsgut* concept is a logically consistent theory, based on a modern, liberal understanding of the function of the state which considers individual human rights as well as needs of society. Its fundamental value lies in the fact that it makes it necessary for the state to justify legislative decisions with reason.

However, the *Rechtsgutstheorie* is not the only concept that can be used to articulate legislative critique. The principle-based approach dominant in the English-speaking discussion could provide a similar structure. Nevertheless, in order for this to constitute critique, the second step needs to be taken. After presenting possible reasons for criminalization, the legitimacy of these reasons needs to be scrutinized. If only one or a few of the limiting principles were well enough developed to form a normative concept which can identify 'good reasons' for criminalization, the Australian discussion could finally have both advantages: a descriptive analysis of historical reasons for criminalization and a normative foundation for critique. It has to be stressed, again, that for this to happen it is not necessary for the vast majority of Australian scholars to have completely agreed on the entirety of the legitimate limits of the criminal law. As with the *Rechtsgutstheorie*, the details of such a concept may be heavily disputed and be the subject of an academic debate on the best solution in particular cases. However, in order to even open up such a debate on the legitimate content of the criminal law among scholars and students (future lawyers, judges and lawmakers) there is a need for there to be a common theme for discussion and a consensus on the argumentative tools to be used in such a discussion and on the authority for lawyers to engage in such normative theorizing. As with normative theories in any area, this will lead to different schools of thought, which will sometimes be similar and lead towards the same end, and sometimes be contradictory.

Some of the interviewees also agreed that the normative structure applied through the *Rechtsgutstheorie* was a possible path for Australian criminal law scholarship:

> So it seems to me that you can structure criminalization around a category of protected interests – property being one and obviously, what is interesting, the changing notions of property over time from a highly tangible to an intangible concept, which explains the rise of IP offences and a whole range of new-data, cyber-crime offences.[With] all these interests, you could develop a list and you can see patterns of criminalization around these, as we would say, 'core interests'. It is a very compelling thesis, I think, to think so. It has not probably been as articulated in our system by the scholars as it is in the German scholarly community because of the distinction and traditions of theorizing around law. But I think the actual core of law is susceptible to those interpretations.[3]

> We could go back to Morris and Hawkins and say that the fundamental purpose of the criminal law is to protect our persons and property. And if it is not

3 Interview with a professor of law at an Australian university (30 August 2007).

> proportionate to that aim it is illegitimate in some way. Certainly, you could make out that sort of argument.[4]

Finally, it was argued that the reason for the lack of a normative concept, and following from that the lack of a normative discussion, is simply due to a missing theorist or school of thought to lead the way:

> I think, in England, Glanville Williams is probably a reason why the criminal law there is in better shape than here. … What he did, he had a normative approach to criminal law. He always looked at the criminal law in two ways. One is: what is the criminal law? The other one is: what ought the criminal law to be? He did not get right into criminalization, but he did have that early article in 1955. I think it is his great books, over several decades, which influenced several generations of practitioners and academics. Certainly his approach is very normative. But Australia has not had someone to take the lead like that. I think, sometimes it is just having someone with an idea. Academic circles are not that big. Rutgers University is good in this area because they have got Douglas Husak there. He is a philosopher who has written quite a bit on morality and the criminal law. And it is that school now that has attracted others who are interested in that because of that one scholar. And as no one has started it here that is maybe why no one is going to follow on.
>
> If someone gets out there and starts the ball rolling it does not take long to get things happening.[5]

Taking both the available normative opinions and the existing trend towards codification in Australia into consideration, the current situation provides a perfect starting position for a discussion of normative concepts regarding the legitimate scope of criminal law.

Providing students with normative concepts and encouraging debates on just solutions can only be beneficial for both the individual law student and for legal culture as a whole. This assessment is independent of the actual conclusions of the concepts that are to be taught. A fundamental characteristic of today's *Rechtsgutstheorie* is the controversial definition of what a *Rechtsgut* actually is. This may be considered a weakness as it seems to merely transfer the discussion on the legitimate scope of the criminal law from the question 'What ought to be criminalized?' to 'What ought to be a *Rechtsgut*?' Critics of the concept may therefore easily claim that all it succeeds in doing is making the discussion more complicated by introducing a new, central term, which apparently does not provide any answers. Such argumentation, despite appearing plausible at first glance, fails to take into consideration that the benefit of the *Rechtsgut* concept is not the postulation of a single criterion that provides the answer to the question

4 Interview with David Brown (Sydney, 13 August 2007).

5 Interview with Dennis Baker (Sydney, 20 August 2007).

of legitimacy for any given offence. In fact, the concept is not able to deliver such clear answers in every case. Its crucial achievement is the establishment of a vocabulary and a structure for legislative critique. While it does not necessarily say which path is the right one to go down, it does provide a guideline on how to choose the right path. Although applying this guideline will still lead to different choices – depending on a person's values and beliefs – it forces the lawmakers to give reasoned explanations for their legislative decisions; a condition that ought to be met in any representative democracy and that every lawyer ought to strive for.

> [I]f academics and to an extent judges are not going to be raising the question of limits, well then, who is? We cannot look to politicians to do so because they do not see it in their interest. They want to use the criminal law as a political weapon whenever they can. That is what they do. Therefore, it is up to judges and academics and lawyers and law reform commissions and so on to raise a way of thinking about the criminal law as a, what I have called, 'limited resource'.[6]

6 Interview with David Brown (Sydney, 13 August 2007).

Bibliography

Amelung, Knut, *Rechtsgüterschutz und Schutz der Gesellschaft* (Protection of *Rechtsgüter* and the Protection of Society) (Athenäum, Frankfurt a.M. 1972).

Amelung, Knut, 'Der Begriff des Rechtsguts in der Lehre vom strafrechtlichen Rechtsgüterschutz' (The Term *Rechtsgut* in the Criminal Law Dogma of the Protection of *Rechtsgüter*), in Roland Hefendehl, Andrew von Hirsch and Wolfgang Wohlers (eds), *Die Rechtsgutstheorie: Legitimationsbasis des Strafrechts oder dogmatisches Glasperlenspiel?* (The *Rechtsgut* Concept: the Basis of Legitimacy for the Criminal Law or a Dogmatic Glass Bead Game?) (Nomos, Baden-Baden 2003) 155.

Anastasopoulou, Ioanna, *Deliktstypen zum Schutz kollektiver Rechtsgüter* (Types of Offences protecting *Rechtsgüter* of the Collective) (C.H. Beck, Munich 2005).

Appel, Ivo, *Verfassung und Strafe, zu den verfassungsrechtlichen Grenzen staatlichen Strafens* (Constitution and Punishment, on the Constitutional Limits of State Punishment) (Duncker & Humblot, Berlin 1998).

Ashworth, Andrew, 'Is the Criminal Law a Lost Cause?' (2000) 116 *Law Quarterly Review* 225.

Ashworth, Andrew, *Principles of Criminal Law* (5th edn Oxford University Press, Oxford 2006).

Australian Law Reform Commission, *Same Crime, Same Time: Sentencing of Federal Offenders*, Report 103 (ALRC, Sydney 2006).

Bagaric, Mirko, 'The "Civil-lisation" of the Criminal Law' (2001) 25 *Criminal Law Journal* 184.

Baker, Dennis J., 'The Moral Limits of Criminalizing Remote Harms' (2007) 10(3) *New Criminal Law Review* 370.

Baker, Dennis J., 'The Harm Principle vs Kantian Criteria for Ensuring Fair, Principled and Just Criminalisation' (2008) 33 *Australian Journal of Legal Philosophy* 1.

Baker, Dennis J., 'The Sense and Nonsense of Criminalising Transfers of Obscene Material' (2008) 26 *Singapore Law Review* 126.

Birnbaum, Johann Michael Franz, 'Über das Erfordernis einer Rechtsverletzung zum Begriff des Verbrechens' (On the Requirement that a Right must be Violated in Order to Constitute a Crime) (1834) (15) *Archiv des Criminalrechts* 149.

Bock, Michael, *Kriminologie, Für Studium und Praxis* (Criminology, For Study and Practice) (3rd edn Verlag Vahlen, Munich 2007).

Bronitt, Simon and McSherry, Bernadette, *Principles of Criminal Law* (2nd edn Thomson Lawbook, Pyrmont 2005).

Brown, David et al., *Brown, Farrier, Neal and Weisbrot's Criminal Laws: Materials and Commentary on Criminal Law and Process of New South Wales* (4th edn The Federation Press, Leichhardt 2006).

Clarkson, C.M.V. and Keating, H.M., *Criminal Law: Text and Materials* (6th edn Sweet & Maxwell, London 2007).

Clough, Jonathan and Mulhern, Carmel, *Criminal Law* (2nd edn LexisNexis Butterworths, Chatswood 2004).

Cook, Catriona et al., *Laying Down the Law* (6th edn LexisNexis Butterworths, Chatswood 2005).

Cramer, Peter and Sternberg-Lieben, Detlev, 'Commentary on § 299' in Schönke, Adolf, Schröder, Horst and Lenckner, Theodor (eds), *Strafgesetzbuch: Kommentar* (Criminal Code: Commentary) (27th edn C.H. Beck, Munich 2006).

Crofts, Penny, *Essential Criminal Law*, Australian Essential Series (3rd edn Cavendish, Coogee 2005).

Devlin, Lord Patrick, *The Enforcement of Morals* (Oxford University Press, London 1965).

Dubber, Markus D., 'The Promise of German Criminal Law: A Science of Crime and Punishment' (2005) 6 *German Law Journal* 1049.

Dubber, Markus D., 'Theories of Crime and Punishment in German Criminal Law' (2006) 53 *American Journal of Comparative Law* 679.

Duff, Antony (ed.), *Philosophy and the Criminal Law: Principle and Critique* (Cambridge Studies in Philosophy and Law) (Cambridge University Press, Cambridge 1998).

Duff, Antony, 'Theories of Criminal Law', *The Stanford Encyclopedia of Philosophy (Fall 2008 Edition)*, Edward N. Zalta (ed.) http://plato.stanford.edu/archives/fall2008/entries/criminal-law/ accessed 19 June 2009.

Dworkin, Gerald, 'Paternalism', *The Stanford Encyclopedia of Philosophy* (Summer 2009 Edition), Zalta, Edward N. (ed.) <http://plato.stanford.edu/archives/sum2009/entries/paternalism/> accessed 19 June 2009.

Dworkin, Ronald, *The Theory and Practice of Autonomy* (Cambridge Studies in Philosophy) (Cambridge University Press, Cambridge 1988).

Dworkin, Ronald et al., 'Assisted Suicide: The Philosophers' Brief' (1997) 44(5) *The New York Review of Books* 41.

Eburn, Michael and Hayes, Robert, *Criminal Law and Procedure in New South Wales* (3rd edn LexisNexis Butterworths, Chatswood 2009).

Edelman, Murray Jacob, *The Symbolic Uses of Politics* (University of Illinois Press, Urbana 1964).

Feinberg, Joel, *The Moral Limits of the Criminal Law* (Oxford University Press, New York 1984–1988).

Feinberg, Joel, *Harm to Others* (Oxford University Press, New York 1984).

Feinberg, Joel, *Offense to Others* (Oxford University Press, New York 1985).

Feinberg, Joel, *Harm to Self* (Oxford University Press, New York 1986).

Feltes, Thomas, Pfeiffer, Christian and Steinhilper, Gernot (eds), *Kriminalpolitik und ihre wissenschaftlichen Grundlagen: Festschrift für Hans-Dieter Schwind zum 70. Geburtstag* (Crime Policy and its Scientific Foundations: Festschrift to Hans-Dieter Schwind for his 70th birthday) (C.F. Müller, Heidelberg 2006).

Findlay, Mark and Hogg, Russell (eds), *Understanding Crime and Criminal Justice* (The Lawbook Company Limited, Sydney 1988).

Findlay, Mark, Odgers, Stephen and Yeo, Stanley, *Australian Criminal Justice* (3rd edn Oxford University Press, Melbourne 2005).

Findlay, Mark, *Criminal Law, Problems in Context* (2nd edn Oxford University Press, Melbourne 2006).

Findlay, Mark and Henham, Ralph, 'Integrating Theory and Method in the Comparative Contextual Analysis of Trial Process', in Mike McConville and Wing Hong Chui (eds), *Research Methods for Law, Research Methods for the Arts and Humanities* (Edinburgh University Press, Edinburgh 2007) 104.

Fisse, Brent, *Howard's Criminal Law* (5th edn The Lawbook Company Limited, Sydney 1990).

Fletcher, George P., *The Grammar of Criminal Law: American, Comparative and International, Volume One, Foundations* (Oxford University Press, New York, Oxford 2007).

Fontana, Andrea and Frey, James H, 'The Interview: From Structured Questions to Negotiated Text' in Norman K. Denzin and Yvonna S. Lincoln (eds), *The Handbook of Qualitative Research* (2nd edn Sage, Thousand Oaks 2000) 645.

Frase, R.S. and Weigend, Thomas, 'German Criminal Justice as a Guide to American Law Reform: Similar Problems, Better Solutions?' (1995) 18 *Boston College International and Comparative Law Review* 317.

Frisch, Wolfgang, 'Rechtsgut, Recht, Deliktsstruktur und Zurechnung im Rahmen der Legitimation staatlichen Strafens' (*Rechtsgut*, Law, Structure of Offences and Attribution within the Framework of the Legitimation of State Punishment), in Roland Hefendehl, Andrew von Hirsch and Wolfgang Wohlers (eds), *Die Rechstgutstheorie: Legitimationsbasis des Strafrechts oder dogmatisches Glasperlenspiel?* (The *Rechtsgut* Concept: the Basis of Legitimacy for the Criminal Law or a Dogmatic Glass Bead Game?) (Nomos, Baden-Baden 2003) 215.

Frisch, Wolfgang, *Strafrecht, Allgemeiner Teil* (Criminal Law, General Part) (Heymanns, Cologne, Berlin, Munich 2009).

Frister, Helmut, *Strafrecht, Allgemeiner Teil, Ein Studienbuch* (Criminal Law, General Part, A Textbook) (4th edn C.H. Beck, Munich 2006).

Führ, Martin, 'Symbolische Gesetzgebung: verfassungswidrig?' (Symbolic Legislation: Unconstitutional?) (2003) *Kritische Vierteljahresschrift für Gesetzgebung und Rechtswissenschaft* (Critical Quarterly Journal for Legislation and Jurisprudence) 5.

Funcke-Auffermann, Niklas, *Symbolische Gesetzgebung im Lichte der positiven Generalprävention, Eine Untersuchung am Beispiel des 'Gesetzes zur Änderung der Vorschriften über die Straftaten gegen die sexuelle Selbstbestimmung und zur Änderung anderer Vorschriften' vom 27. Dezember 2003* (Symbolic Legislation in the Light of the Theory of Positive General Deterrence, An Analysis Taking as an Example the 'Act on the Revision of the Provisions on Crimes against Sexual Self-Determination and other Provisions' of 27 December 2003) (Duncker & Humblot, Berlin 2007).

Gillies, Peter, *Criminal Law* (4th edn LBC Information Services, North Ryde 1997).

Goode, M.R., 'Codification of the Australian Criminal Law' (1992) 16 *Criminal Law Journal* 5.

Goode, M.R., 'Constructing Criminal Law Reform and the Model Criminal Code' (2002) 26 *Criminal Law Journal* 152.

Graf von Bernstorff, Christoph, *Einführung in das Englische Recht* (Introduction to English Law) (3rd edn C.H. Beck, Munich 2006).

Gropp, Walter, *Strafrecht, Allgemeiner Teil* (Criminal Law, General Part) (3rd edn Springer, Berlin 2005).

Gross, Hyman, *A Theory of Criminal Justice* (Oxford University Press, New York 1979).

Gutmann, Thomas, 'Der eigene Tod – Die Selbstbestimmung des Patienten und der Schutz des Lebens in ethischer und rechtlicher Dimension' (One's own Death – The Autonomy of the Patient and the Protection of Life in the Ethical and Legal Dimension) (2002) *Ethik in der Medizin* 170.

Hart, H.L.A., *Punishment and Responsibility, Essays in the Philosophy of Law* (Clarendon Press, Oxford 1968).

Hassemer, Winfried, *Theorie und Soziologie des Verbrechens. Ansätze zu einer praxisorientierten Rechtsgutslehre* (Theory and Sociology of Crime. Approaches to a Practice-oriented *Rechtsgut* Concept) (Athenäum, Frankfurt a.M. 1973).

Hassemer, Winfried, *Einführung in die Grundlagen des Strafrechts* (Introduction to the Foundations of Criminal Law) (JuS-Schriftenreihe, 2nd edn C.H. Beck, Munich 1990)

Hassemer, Winfried, 'Vielfalt und Wandel. Offene Horizonte eines interkulturellen Strafrechts' (Diversity and Change. The Open Horizons of Intercultural Criminal Law), in Otfried Höffe (ed.), *Gibt es ein interkulturelles Strafrecht?* (Does Intercultural Criminal Law exist?) (Suhrkamp, Frankfurt a.M. 1999) 157.

Hassemer, Winfried, *Strafen im Rechtsstaat* (Punishment in the Constitutional State) Strafrechtswissenschaft und Strafrechtspolitik, Band 3 (Nomos, Baden-Baden 2000).

Hassemer, Winfried, 'Darf es Straftaten geben, die ein strafrechtliches Rechtsgut nicht in Mitleidenschaft ziehen?' (May there be Criminal Offences that do not affect a *Rechtsgut*?), in Roland Hefendehl, Andrew von Hirsch and Wolfgang Wohlers (eds), *Die Rechstgutstheorie: Legitimationsbasis des Strafrechts oder dogmatisches Glasperlenspiel?* (The *Rechtsgut* Concept: The Basis of

Legitimacy for the Criminal Law or a Dogmatic Glass Bead Game?) (Nomos, Baden-Baden 2003) 57.

Hassemer, Winfried and Neumann, Ulfried, 'Kommentierung zu § 1 StGB' in Urs Kindhäuser, Ulfrid Neumann and Hans-Ullrich Paeffgen (eds), *Strafgesetzbuch, Nomos-Kommentar* (2nd edn Nomos, Baden-Baden 2005).

Hefendehl, Roland, *Kollektive Rechtsgüter im Strafrecht* (Collective Legal Goods/ Interests in the Criminal Law) (Heymanns, Cologne, Berlin, Munich 2002).

Hefendehl, Roland, von Hirsch, Andrew and Wohlers, Wolfgang (eds), *Die Rechtsgutstheorie: Legitimationsbasis des Strafrechts oder dogmatisches Glasperlenspiel?* (The *Rechtsgut* Concept: the Basis of Legitimacy for the Criminal Law or a Dogmatic Glass Bead Game?) (Nomos, Baden-Baden 2003).

Hefendehl, Roland, 'Das Rechtsgut als materialer Angelpunkt einer Strafnorm' (The *Rechtsgut* as the Substantive Lynchpin of a Criminal Offence), in Roland Hefendehl, Andrew von Hirsch and Wolfgang Wohlers (eds), *Die Rechstgutstheorie: Legitimationsbasis des Strafrechts oder dogmatisches Glasperlenspiel?* (The *Rechtsgut* Concept: the Basis of Legitimacy for the Criminal Law or a Dogmatic Glass Bead Game?) (Nomos, Baden-Baden 2003) 119.

Hefendehl, Roland, 'Mit langem Atem: Der Begriff des Rechtsguts – Oder: Was seit dem Erscheinen des Sammelbandes über die Rechtsgutstheorie geschah' (With Tenacity: The Concept of *Rechtsgut* – Or: What has happened since the Publication of the Anthology on the *Rechtsgut* Concept) (2007) *Goltdammers Archiv für Strafrecht* 1.

Hefendehl, Roland, *Inzestverbot: BVerfG nimmt sich Auszeit und erklärt sich für das Strafrecht nicht für zuständig*, (The Prohibition Against Incest: Federal Constitutional Court takes Time-out and Declares it is Not Responsible for Criminal Law) (13 March 2008) <http://www.smartnuts.com/index.php/main/inzestverbot_bverfg_nimmt_sich_eine_auszeit_uun_erklaert_sich_fuer_das_stra/> accessed 19 June 2009.

Heine, Günter, 'Commentary on § 299', in Adolf Schönke, Horst Schröder and Thedor Lenckner (eds), *Strafgesetzbuch: Kommentar* (Criminal Code: Commentary) (27th edn C.H. Beck, Munich 2006).

Höffe, Otfried, *Gibt es ein interkulturelles Strafrecht?* (Does Intercultural Criminal Law Exist?) (Suhrkamp, Frankfurt a.M. 1999).

Hörnle, Tatjana, 'Penal Law and Sexuality: Recent Reforms in German Criminal Law' (2000) *Buffalo Criminal Law Review* 639.

Hörnle, Tatjana, 'Offensive Behaviour and German Criminal Law' (2001) *Buffalo Criminal Law Review* 255.

Hörnle, Tatjana, 'Der Schutz von Gefühlen im StGB' (The Protection of Feelings in the Criminal Code), in Roland Hefendehl, Andrew von Hirsch and Wolfgang Wohlers (eds), *Die Rechstgutstheorie: Legitimationsbasis des Strafrechts oder dogmatisches Glasperlenspiel?* (The *Rechtsgut* Concept: the Basis of

Legitimacy for the Criminal Law or a Dogmatic Glass Bead Game?) (Nomos, Baden-Baden 2003) 268.

Hörnle, Tatjana, *Grob anstößiges Verhalten, strafrechtlicher Schutz von Moral, Gefühlen und Tabus* (Grossly Offensive Behaviour, The Protection of Morality, Feelings and Taboos by the Criminal Law) (Klostermann, Frankfurt a.M. 2005).

Hörnle, Tatjana, 'Das Verbot des Geschwisterinzests – Verfassungsgerichtliche Bestätigung und verfassungsrechtliche Kritik' (The Prohibition of Incest between Siblings – Confirmation by the Constitutional Court and Critique based on Constitutional Law) (2008) *Neue Juristische Wochenschrift* 2085.

Hörnle, Tatjana, *Inzest-Urteil – 'Das Verbot ist nicht plausibel' – Spiegel – Interview mit Professorin Tatjana Hörnle* (The Incest-judgment – 'The Prohibition is Implausible' – Spiegel-Interview with Professor Tatjana Hörnle*)* (15 March 2008) Spiegel Online <http://www.spiegel.de/panorama/justiz/0,1518,541628,00.html> accessed 19 June 2009.

Hufen, Friedhelm and Jahn, Matthias, 'Anmerkung zu BVerfG, NJW 2008, 1137 (Commentary on BVerfG, NJW 2008, 1137) (2008) *Juristiche Schulung* 550.

Husak, Douglas, *Philosophy of Criminal Law* (Rowman & Littlefield, Totowa 1987).

Husak, Douglas, *Drugs and Rights* (Cambridge Studies in Philosophy and Public Policy) (Cambridge University Press, Cambridge 1992).

Husak, Douglas, *Overcriminalization: The Limits of the Criminal Law* (Oxford University Press, Oxford, New York 2008).

Jäger, Herbert, *Strafgesetzgebung und Rechtsgüterschutz bei den Sittlichkeitsdelikten, Eine kriminalsoziologische Untersuchung* (Criminal Legislation and the Protection of *Rechtsgüter* with regard to Crimes against Morality, An Analysis based on Criminal Sociology) (Enke, Stuttgart 1957).

Jakobs, Günther, 'Bürgerstrafrecht und Feindstrafrecht' (Criminal Law for the Citizen and Criminal Law for the Enemy), in Yu-hsiu Hsu (ed.), *Foundations and Limits of Criminal Law and Criminal Procedure – An Anthology in Memory of Professor Fu-Tsen Hung* (Taipei 2003) 41.

Jakobs, Günter, 'Was schützt das Strafrecht: Rechtsgüter oder Normgeltung?' (What Does the Criminal Law Protect: *Rechtsgüter* or the Standing of Norms?) in Takayuki Shiibashi (ed.), *Festschrift für Seiji Saito* (Tokyo 2003) 17.

Jescheck, Hans-Heinrich and Weigend, Thomas, *Lehrbuch des Strafrechts: Allgemeiner Teil* (Textbook on Criminal Law: General Part) (5th edn Duncker & Humblot, Berlin 1996).

Jescheck, Hans-Heinrich, 'Einleitung' (Introduction), in Burkhard Jähnke, Heinrich Wilhelm Laufhütte and Walter Odersky (eds), *Strafgesetzbuch, Leipziger Kommentar, Großkommentar, Erster Band, Einleitung, §§ 1 bis 31* (Criminal Code, Leipzig Commentary, Great Commentary, First Volume, Introduction, §§ 1–31*)* (11th edn De Gruyter, Berlin).

Joecks, Wolfgang, 'Kommentierung zu § 1 StGB' (Annotations on § 1 Criminal Code), in Wolfgang Joecks and Klaus Miebach (eds), *Münchener Kommentar zum Strafgesetzbuch* (Munich Commentary on the Criminal Code) (C.H. Beck, Munich 2003).

Joecks, Wolfgang, *Studienkommentar StGB* (Study Commentary on the Criminal Code) (8th edn C.H. Beck, Munich 2009).

Junge, Iris, *Das Schutzgut des § 130 StGB* (The protected good/interest of § 130 of the Criminal Code) (GCA, Augsburg 2000).

Kaiafa-Gbandi, Maria, 'Ein Blick auf Brennpunkte der Entwicklung der deutschen Strafrechtsdogmatik vor der Jahrtausendwende aus der Sicht eines Mitglieds der griechischen Strafrechtswissenschaft' (A Review of the Focal Points in the Development of German Doctrines of Criminal Law before the Turn of the Millennium from the Point of View of a Member of the Greek Criminal Jurisprudential Community), in Albin Eser, Winfried Hassemer and Björn Burkhardt (eds), *Die deutsche Strafrechtswissenschaft vor der Jahrtausendwende* (German Criminal Jurisprudence before the Turn of the Century) (C.H. Beck, Munich 2000) 261.

Kaufmann, Arthur, 'Euthanasie – Selbsttötung – Tötung auf Verlangen' (Euthanasia – Suicide – Killing Someone at their Request) (1983) *Medizinrecht* 121.

Kindhäuser, Urs, *Strafrecht, Allgemeiner Teil* (Criminal Law, General Part) (3rd edn, Nomos, Baden-Baden 2008).

Kirby, Justice Michael, 'Criminal Law Futurology' (2005) 17(1) *Current Issues in Criminal Justice* 122.

Krey, Volker, *Deutsches Strafrecht, Allgemeiner Teil, Band 1, Grundlagen, Tatbestandsmäßigkeit, Rechtswidrigkeit, Schuld* (German Criminal Law, General Part, Volume 1, Foundations, Elements of Offences, Unlawfulness, Culpability) (3rd edn Kohlhammer, Stuttgart 2008).

Kühl, Kristian, *Strafrecht, Allgemeiner Teil* (Criminal Law, General Part) (6th edn Vahlen, Munich 2008).

Lacey, Nicola, *State Punishment: Political Principles and Community Values* (Routledge, London 1988).

Lacey, Nicola, 'Contingency, Coherence, and Conceptualism: Reflections on the Encounter between "Critique" and "Philosophy" of the Criminal Law', in Antony Duff (ed.), *Philosophy and the Criminal Law: Principle and Critique* (Cambridge Studies in Philosophy and Law) (Cambridge University Press, Cambridge 1998) 9.

Lacey, Nicola, 'Legal Constructions of Crime', in Mike Maguire, Rod Morgan and Robert Reiner (eds), *The Oxford Handbook of Criminology* (3rd edn Oxford University Press, Oxford 2002) 282.

Lacey, Nicola, Wells, Celia and Quick, Oliver, *Reconstructing Criminal Law: Text and Materials* (3rd edn LexisNexis Butterworths, London 2003).

Lackner, Karl and Kühl, Kristian, *Strafgesetzbuch, Kommentar* (Criminal Code, Commentary) (26th edn C.H. Beck, Munich 2007).

Lagodny, Otto, *Strafrecht vor den Schranken der Grundrechte, die Ermächtigung zum strafrechtlichen Vorwurf im Lichte der Grundrechtsdogmatik; dargestellt am Beispiel der Vorfeldkriminalisierung* (Criminal Law and Constitutional

Constraints, the Authorization for a Criminal Charge in the Light of the Basic Rights Doctrine; illustrated by using Criminalization of Preparatory Acts as an Example) (Mohr, Tübingen 1996).

Lanham, David et al., *Criminal Laws in Australia* (The Federation Press, Annandale 2006).

Lauterwein, Carl Constantin, *Symbolische Gesetzgebung: Eine Untersuchung am Beispiel Strafrecht* (Symbolic Legislation: An Analysis using Criminal Law as an Example) (Junge Wissenschaft, Schriften der Hochschule für Politik München, Band 10) (Vögel, Munich 2006).

Lundstedt, Anders Vilhelm, *Legal Thinking Revised: My Views on Law* (Almqvist and Wiksell, Stockholm 1956).

Mansdörfer, Marco (ed.), *Die allgemeine Straftatlehre des Common Law: Eine Darstellung unter besonderer Berücksichtigung des englischen Strafrechts* (The General Concept of Crime in the Common Law: A Description with Particular Consideration of the English Criminal Law) (C.F. Müller, Heidelberg 2005).

Mason, Sir Anthony, 'Law and Morality' (1995) 4 *Griffith Law Review* 147.

Marx, Michael, *Zur Definition des Begriffs 'Rechtsgut', Prolegomena einer materialen Verbrechenslehre* (On the Definition of the Term *Rechtsgut*, Prolegomena to a Substantive Concept of Crime) (Heymanns, Cologne, Berlin, Munich 1972).

McCutcheon, Paul, 'Morality and the Criminal Law: Reflections on Hart-Devlin' (2002) 47 *Criminal Law Quarterly* 15.

Meier, Bernd-Dieter, *Kriminologie* (Criminology) (3rd edn C.H. Beck, Munich 2007).

McSherry, Bernadette and Naylor, Bronwyn, *Australian Criminal Law: Critical Perspectives* (Oxford University Press, Melbourne 2004).

Mill, John Stuart, *On Liberty* (first published 1859, Penguin, London 1985).

Naucke, Wolfgang, 'Schwerpunktverlagerungen im Strafrecht' (Shifting of Focus in Criminal Law) (1993) *Kritische Vierteljahresschrift für Gesetzgebung und Rechtswissenschaft* (Critical Quarterly Journal for Legislation and Jurisprudence) 135.

Nestler, Cornelius, 'Constitutional Principles, Criminal Law Principles and German Drug Law' (1998) *Buffalo Criminal Law Review* 661.

Newig, Jens, *Symbolische Umweltgesetzgebung, Rechtssoziologische Untersuchungen am Beispiel des Ozongesetzes, des Kreislaufwirtschafts- und Abfallgesetzes sowie der Großfeuerungsanlagenverordnung* (Symbolic Environmental Legislation, Socio-Legal Analyses Taking as Examples the Ozone Act, the Closed Substance Cycle and Waste Management Act and the Large Combustion Plants Act) (Duncker & Humblot, Berlin 2003).

Norrie, Alan, *Law, Ideology and Punishment: Retrieval and Critique of the Liberal Ideal of Criminal Justice* (Kluwer, Dordrecht 1991).

Norrie, Alan, *Crime, Reason and History: A Critical Introduction to Criminal Law* (Law in Context) (2nd edn Cambridge University Press, Cambridge 2001).

Odgers, Stephen, 'Book Review. Principles of Criminal Law by Simon Bronitt and Bernadette McSherry. LBC Information Services 2001' (2001) *Summer 2001/2002 NSW Bar News* 66.

Otto, Harro, *Grundkurs Strafrecht, Allgmeine Strafrechtslehre* (Basic Course Criminal Law, General Criminal Law Doctrine) (7th edn De Gruyter, Berlin 2004).

Otto, Harro, *Grundkurs Strafrecht, Die einzelnen Delikte* (Basic Course Criminal Law, The Individual Offences) (7th edn De Gruyter, Berlin 2005).

Packer, Herbert L., *The Limits of the Criminal Sanction* (Stanford University Press, Stanford 1968).

Padfield, Nicola, *Criminal Law* (5th edn Oxford University Press, Oxford, New York 2006).

Papageorgiou, Konstantinos A., *Schaden und Strafe, Auf dem Weg zu einer Theorie der strafrechtlichen Moralität* (Harm and Punishment, On the Road to a Theory of Criminal Law Morality) (Nomos, Baden-Baden 1994).

Preston, Justice Brian J., 'Principled Sentencing for Environmental Offences – Part 1: Purposes of Sentencing' (2007) 31 *Criminal Law Journal* 91.

Puppe, Ingeborg, *Strafrecht, Allgemeiner Teil im Spiegel der Rechtsprechung, Band I, Die Lehre vom Tatbestand, Rechtswidrigkeit, Schuld* (Criminal Law, General Part in the Mirror of the Judicature, Volume I, The Doctrine of Elements of a Crime, Unlawfulness, Culpability) (Nomos, Baden-Baden 2002).

Puppe, Ingeborg, *Strafrecht, Allgemeiner Teil im Spiegel der Rechtsprechung, Band 2, Sonderformen des Verbrechens* (Criminal Law, General Part in the Mirror of the Judicature, Volume II, Special Forms of Criminal Behaviour) (Nomos, Baden-Baden 2005).

Rengier, Rudolf, *Strafrecht, Allgemeiner Teil* (Criminal Law, General Part) (C.H. Beck, Munich 2009).

Roxin, Claus, 'Sinn und Grenzen staatlicher Strafe' (The Purpose and Limits of State Punishment) (1966) *Juristische Schulung* 377.

Roxin, Claus, 'Crime Policy and the Criminal Law System', trans. J. Fosberry, in Institute for Scientific Co-operation (ed.), *Law and State, A Biannual Collection of Recent German Contributions to these Fields*, Volume 6 (Göbel, Tübingen 1972) 32.

Roxin, Claus, 'Wandlungen der Strafrechtswissenschaft' (Transformations of Legal Science) (1980) *Juristische Arbeitsblätter* 545.

Roxin, Claus, *Strafrecht, Allgemeiner Teil, Band I: Grundlagen, Aufbau der Verbrechenslehre* (Criminal law, General Part, Volume I: Foundations, Structure of the Concept of Crime) (3rd edn C.H. Beck, Munich 1997).

Roxin, Claus, *Strafverfahrensrecht* (The Law of Criminal Procedure) (25th edn C.H. Beck, Munich 1998).

Roxin, Claus, *Höchstrichterliche Rechtsprechung zum Allgemeinen Teil des Strafrechts, 100 Entscheidungen für Studium und Referendariat mit Fragen und Antworten* (Case Law of the Highest Courts on the General Part of the

Criminal Law, 100 Judgements for Study and Clerkship with Questions and Answers) (C.H. Beck, Munich 1998).

Roxin, Claus, *Strafrecht, Allgemeiner Teil, Band I: Grundlagen, Aufbau der Verbrechenslehre* (Criminal Law, General Part, Volume I: Foundations, Structure of the Concept of Crime) (4th edn C.H. Beck, Munich 2006).

Roxin, Claus, *Täterschaft und Tatherrschaft* (Commission of the Offence and Control over the Offence) (6th edn De Gruyter, Berlin 2006).

Roxin, Claus, 'Zur neueren Entwicklung der Rechtsgutsdebatte' (On the Latest Developments in the Debate on the *Rechtsgut* Concept), in *Festschrift für Winfried Hassemer* (forthcoming in 2010).

Roxin, Claus and Achenbach, Hans, *Strafprozessrecht* (The Law of Criminal Procedure) (16th edn C.H. Beck, Munich 2006).

Roxin, Claus, Arzt, Gunther and Tiedemann, Klaus, *Einführung in das Strafrecht und Strafprozessrecht* (Introduction to Criminal Law and Law of Criminal Procedure) (5th edn C.F. Müller, Heidelberg 2006).

Rudolphi, Hans-Joachim, 'Die verschiedenen Aspekte des Rechtsgutsbegriffs' (The Different Aspects of the *Rechtsgut* Concept), in Juristische Fakultät der Georg-August-Univeristät Göttingen (ed.), *Festschrift für Richard M. Honig* (Schwarz, Göttingen 1970) 151.

Rudolphi, Hans-Joachim, 'Kommentierung zu § 1 StGB' (Annotations on § 1 Criminal Code), in Hans-Joachim Rudolphi, Eckhard Horn and Erich Samson (eds), *Systematischer Kommentar zum Strafgesetzbuch, Band 1, Allgemeiner Teil, §§ 1–79b* (Systematic Commentary on the Criminal Code, Volume 1, General Part, §§ 1–79b) (7th edn, Luchterhand, Neuwied 2008).

Rush, Peter, *Criminal Law* (Butterworths Casebook Companions) (Butterworths, Sydney 1997).

Rush, Peter, McVeigh, Shaun and Young, Alison (eds), *Criminal Legal Doctrine* (Ashgate, Aldershot 1997).

Rush, Peter and Yeo, Stanley M.H., *Criminal Law Sourcebook* (2nd edn LexisNexis Butterworths, Chatswood 2006).

Schmidt, Rolf, *Strafrecht, Allgemeiner Teil, Grundlagen der Strafbarkeit, Aufbau des strafrechtlichen Gutachtens* (Criminal Law, General Part, Foundations of Criminal Responsibility, Structure of a Criminal Law Opinion) (6th edn Verlag Rolf Schmidt, Grasberg 2007).

Schönke, Adolf, Schröder, Horst and Lenckner, Theodor (eds), *Strafgesetzbuch: Kommentar* (Criminal Code: Commentary) (27th edn C.H. Beck, Munich 2006).

Schonsheck, Jonathan, *On Criminalization: An Essay in the Philosophy of the Criminal Law* (Kluwer, Dordrecht 1994).

Schulenberg, Johanna, 'Dogmatische Zusammenhänge von Rechtsgut, Deliktsstruktur und objektiver Zurechnung' (Dogmatic Correlations of *Rechtsgut*, Structure of Offences and Objective Attribution), in Roland Hefendehl, Andrew von Hirsch and Wolfgang Wohlers (eds), *Die Rechtsgutstheorie: Legitimationsbasis des Strafrechts oder dogmatisches*

Glasperlenspiel? (The *Rechtsgut* Concept: The Basis of Legitimacy for the Criminal Law or a Dogmatic Glass Bead Game?) (Nomos, Baden-Baden 2003) 244.

Schünemann, Bernd, 'Principles of Criminal Legislation in Postmodern Society: The Case of Environmental Law' (1997) *Buffalo Criminal Law Review* 175.

Schünemann, Bernd, 'Das Rechtsgüterschutzprinzip als Fluchtpunkt der verfassungsrechtlichen Grenzen der Straftatbestände und ihrer Interpretation' (The Principle of the Protection of *Rechtsgüter* as the Junction between the Constitutional Limits of Criminal Offences and the Interpretation of Criminal Offences), in Roland Hefendehl, Andrew von Hirsch and Wolfgang Wohlers (eds), *Die Rechtsgutstheorie: Legitimationsbasis des Strafrechts oder dogmatisches Glasperlenspiel?* (The *Rechtsgut* Concept: The Basis of Legitimacy for the Criminal Law or a Dogmatic Glass Bead Game?) (Nomos, Baden-Baden 2003) 133.

Schwind, Hans-Dieter, *Kriminologie, eine praxisorientierte Einführung mit Beispielen* (Criminology, a Practice-oriented Introduction with Examples) (19th edn Kriminalistik-Verlag, Heidelberg, Munich 2009).

Seelmann, Kurt, 'Rechtsgutskonzept, "Harm Principle" und Anerkennungsmodell als Strafwürdigkeitskriterien' (The *Rechtsgut* Concept, 'Harm Principle' and Recognition Model as Criteria for Legitimate Criminalization), in Roland Hefendehl, Andrew von Hirsch and Wolfgang Wohlers (eds), *Die Rechtsgutstheorie: Legitimationsbasis des Strafrechts oder dogmatisches Glasperlenspiel?* (The *Rechtsgut* Concept: the Basis of Legitimacy for the Criminal Law or a Dogmatic Glass Bead Game?) (Nomos, Baden-Baden 2003) 261.

Seher, Gerhard, 'Prinzipiengestützte Strafnormlegitimation und der Rechtsgutbegriff' (Principle-based Legitimation of Criminal Offences and the *Rechtsgut* Concept), in Roland Hefendehl, Andrew von Hirsch and Wolfgang Wohlers (eds), *Die Rechstgutstheorie: Legitimationsbasis des Strafrechts oder dogmatisches Glasperlenspiel?* (The *Rechtsgut* Concept: the Basis of Legitimacy for the Criminal Law or a Dogmatic Glass Bead Game?) (Nomos Baden-Baden 2003) 39.

Sexton, Michael and Maher, Laurence W., *The Legal Mystique: The Role of Lawyers in Australian Society* (Angus & Robertson Publishers, Sydney1982).

Shute, Stephen and Simester, A.P. (eds), *Criminal Law Theory: Doctrines of the General Part* (Oxford Monographs on Criminal Law and Justice) (Oxford University Press, New York 2002).

Simester, A.P. and Smith, A.T.H. (eds), *Harm and Culpability* (Oxford Monographs on Criminal Law and Justice) (Clarendon Press, Oxford 1996).

Simester, A.P. and Sullivan, G.R., *Criminal Law: Theory and Doctrine* (2nd edn Hart Publishing, Oxford 2003).

Simester, A.P. and von Hirsch, Andrew, 'Rethinking the Offense Principle' (2002) 8 *Legal Theory* 269.

Sina, Peter, *Die Dogmengeschichte des strafrechtlichen Begriffs 'Rechtsgut'* (The History of Dogma of the Criminal Law Concept of *Rechtsgut*) (Helbing & Lichtenhahn, Basel 1962).

Stächelin, Gregor, *Strafgesetzgebung im Verfassungsstaat* (Criminal Legislation in the Constitutional State) (Duncker & Humblodt, Berlin 1998).

Staff Writers, www.news.com.au, Incest couple John and Jenny Deaves's first child died (7 April 2008) <http://www.news.com.au/story/0,23599,23494953-2,00.html> accessed 19 June 2009.

Stanton-Ife, John, 'The Limits of Law', *The Stanford Encyclopedia of Philosophy (Winter 2008 Edition)*, Edward N. Zalta (ed.) <http://plato.stanford.edu/archives/win2008/entries/law-limits/> accessed 19 June 2009.

Stratenwerth, Günter, 'Kriminalisierung bei Delikten gegen Kollektivrechtsgüter' (Criminalization of Offences against *Rechtsgüter* belonging to the Collective), in Roland Hefendehl, Andrew von Hirsch and Wolfgang Wohlers (eds), *Die Rechtsgutstheorie: Legitimationsbasis des Strafrechts oder dogmatisches Glasperlenspiel?* (The *Rechtsgut* Concept: the Basis of Legitimacy for the Criminal Law or a Dogmatic Glass Bead Game?) (Nomos, Baden-Baden 2003) 255.

Stratenwerth, Günter and Kuhlen, Lothar, *Strafrecht, Allgemeiner Teil, Band 1, Die Straftat* (Criminal Law, General Part, Volume 1, The Offence) (5th edn Heymanns, Cologne, Berlin, Munich 2004).

Tiedemann, Klaus, *Tatbestandsfunktionen im Nebenstrafrecht* (Functions of the Criminal Offences that are not Regulated in the Criminal Code) (Mohr, Tübingen 1969).

Tröndle, Herbert and Fischer, Thomas, *Strafgesetzbuch und Nebengesetze* (Criminal Code and Supplementary Laws) (50th edn C.H. Beck, Munich 2001).

von Hirsch, Andrew, 'The Offence Principle in Criminal Law' (2000) *King's College Law Review* 78.

von Hirsch, Andrew, 'Der Rechtsgutsbegriff und das "Harm Principle"' (The *Rechtsgut* Concept and the 'Harm Principle'), in Roland Hefendehl, Andrew von Hirsch and Wolfgang Wohlers (eds), *Die Rechtsgutstheorie: Legitimationsbasis des Strafrechts oder dogmatisches Glasperlenspiel?* (The *Rechtsgut* Concept: the Basis of Legitimacy for the Criminal Law or a Dogmatic Glass Bead Game?) (Nomos, Baden-Baden 2003) 13.

Voss, Monika, *Symbolische Gesetzgebung, Fragen zur Rationalität von Strafgesetzgebungsakten* (Symbolic Legislation, Questions on the Rationality of Acts of Criminal Legislation) (Gremer, Ebelsbach 1989).

Waller, L. and Williams, C.R., *Criminal Law: Texts and Cases* (10th edn LexisNexis Butterworths, Chatswood 2005).

Weber, Ulrich, Baumann, Jürgen and Mitsch, Wolfgang, *Strafrecht, Allgemeiner Teil, Lehrbuch* (Criminal Law, General Law, Textbook) (11th edn Gieseking, Bielefeld 2005).

Welzel, Hans, *Das deutsche Strafrecht* (German Criminal Law) (11th edn De Gruyter, Berlin 1969).

Wessels, Johannes and Beulke, Werner, *Strafrecht, Allgemeiner Teil, Die Straftat und ihr Aufbau* (Criminal Law, General Part, The Offence and its Structure) (38th edn C.F. Müller, Heidelberg 2008).

Wessels, Johannes and Hettinger, Michael, *Strafrecht, Besonderer Teil 1, Straftaten gegen Persönlichkeits- und Gemeinschaftswerte* (Criminal Law, Special Part 1, Crimes against Interests of Personality and of the Collective) (32nd edn C.F. Müller, Heidelberg 2008).

Wessels, Johannes and Hillenkamp, Thomas, *Strafrecht, Besonderer Teil 2, Straftaten gegen Vermögenswerte* (Criminal Law, Special Part 2, Crimes against Property Assets) (31st edn C.F. Müller, Heidelberg 2008).

Williams, Glanville, *Textbook of Criminal Law* (Stevens & Sons, London 1983).

Wilson, Geoffrey, 'Comparative Legal Scholarship', in Mike McConville and Wing Hong Chui (eds), *Research Methods for Law, Research Methods for the Arts and Humanities* (Edinburgh University Press, Edinburgh 2007) 87.

Wohlers, Wolfgang, *Deliktstypen des Präventionsstrafrechts – zur Dogmatik 'moderner' Gefährdungsdelikte* (Types of Offences in the Preventive Criminal Law – on the Dogmatics of 'Modern' Offences of Endangerment) (Duncker & Humblot, Berlin 2000).

Woods, G.D., *A History of Criminal Law in New South Wales: The Colonial Period 1788–1900* (The Federation Press, Leichhardt 2002).

Yeo, Stanley, 'Learning from the Japanese Approach to Criminal Responsibility' (2003) 27 *Criminal Law Journal* 180.

Zabel, Benno 'Die Grenzen des Tabuschutzes im Strafrecht' (The Limits of the Protection of Taboos in the Criminal Law) (2008) *Juristische Rundschau* 453.

Ziethen, Jörg, 'Anmerkung zu BVerfG, NJW 2008, 1137' (Commentary on BVerfG, NJW 2008, 1137) (2008) *Neue Zeitschrift für Strafrecht* 617.

Zipf, Heinz, *Kriminalpolitik: Ein Lehrbuch* (Crime Policy: A Textbook) (2nd edn C.F. Müller, Heidelberg 1980).

Appendix A

Interview Questions

General Questions

1. In general, what do you understand by 'the limits of criminal law'?
2. I am sure you are familiar with the harm principle. What do you think is or are the valid principle(s) for determining legitimate invasions of liberty, so that no conduct that fails to satisfy its or their terms can properly be made criminal?
3. If there is more than one limiting principle, are they all of equal weight? Is any of them sufficient reason for criminalization?
4. In Germany, the limits of criminal law are deduced from its general purpose. Do you think that this kind of limiting principle(s) we were just talking about could be deduced from a general purpose of criminal law?

Sources of Theory

5. What role do academics/judges/law reform commissions play in the discussion on the limits of criminal law in Australia?
6. Australian criminal law textbooks, as well as judgements and law reform documents, almost do not deal with this question at all. Why do Australian academics/judges/law reformers not seem to be interested in establishing such normative theories?

Individual Offences

7. Do the offences of sexual intercourse between consenting adult relatives (which is punishable as incest) and bestiality meet the terms of the principle(s) so that this conduct is legitimately criminalized?
8. Which principle(s) can justify the criminalization of self-administration of illicit drugs?
9. The offence of sexual assault is considered to protect against harm. How does consent, in general, affect that notion?
10. Are there any (other) existing offences which in your opinion do not meet the terms of the principle(s) and therefore should not be criminal offences?

Joel Feinberg

11. Are you familiar with Joel Feinberg's work on the limits of criminal law? And if that is the case, what do you think of his theory?

Appendix B

Interviewees

Dennis Baker, at the time of the interview, Lecturer in Law, University of Western Sydney; today, Lecturer in Law, King's College London. Interviewed at his office in Sydney, 20 August 2007.

Sir Gerard Brennan AC KBE, former Chief Justice of Australia. Interviewed at his chambers in Sydney, 15 August 2007.

David Brown, Emeritus Professor of Law, University of New South Wales. Interviewed at his office in Sydney, 13 August 2007.

Nicholas Cowdery AM QC, Director of Public Prosecutions New South Wales. Interviewed at his office in Sydney, 13 August 2007.

Brent Fisse, Solicitor and former Professor of Law at the University of Sydney. Interviewed at his house in Sydney, 22 August 2007.

Matthew Goode, Managing Solicitor, Legislation and Legal Policy, Policy, Planning and Legislation, Attorney-General's Department of South Australia. Interviewed at his office in Adelaide, 14 August 2007.

Sir Michael Kirby AC CMG, former Justice of the High Court of Australia (until 2 February 2009). Interviewed at his chambers in Sydney, 24 July 2007.

Ian Leader-Elliott, Associate Professor of Law, University of Adelaide. Interviewed at his office in Adelaide, 14 August 2007.

Stephen Odgers SC, Barrister. Interviewed at his chambers in Sydney, 27 August 2007.

David Weisbrot AM, Emeritus Professor of Law, President of the Australian Law Reform Commission. Interviewed at his office in Sydney, 12 September 2007.

Professor of law at an Australian university. This interviewee wishes not to be identified in the book. Interviewed at his office, 30 August 2007.

Index

Kolibri 360 GmbH
Ferdinand-Jühlke-Straße 7
99095 Erfurt, Deutschland
produktsicherheit@kolibri360.de